T0333764

Resilient Organizations

Recent financial crises have shown that firms need to create more robust business models. However, it seems that the task of developing resilience – a firm's ability to adapt, endure, bounce back and then thrive, despite the shock – appears on most managers' strategic issue list only after such a shock has occurred. Managers, through responsible leadership, can make explicit choices that will enhance their firm's resilience, increasing their chances of anticipating and avoiding these shocks. This book is the result of a three-year research project across seven industries, and is aimed at improving the understanding of why some firms are better than others in dealing with market turbulence. Pirotti and Venzin develop a measure for organizational resilience, identifying resilience drivers and demonstrating how firms can appropriate value from high-resilience levels. It is a valuable read for graduates taking a course in strategy and global management, and for reflective practitioners.

Guia Beatrice Pirotti is SDA Bocconi Professor of Strategic and Entrepreneurial Management and teaches business strategy at Bocconi University. She has a PhD in business administration and management, Bocconi University, and was visiting scholar at Emory University, Atlanta, USA in 2009. Her areas of expertise include organizational resilience, strategic planning and competitiveness of firms. She regularly writes for *Ideas of Management on Strategy and Entrepreneurship*, SDA Bocconi School of Management, and she is co-author of the book *Resilience* (2014).

Markus Venzin is Professor of Global Strategy at Bocconi University and Director of Research Division at SDA Bocconi, specializing in global strategy, strategic planning and organizational resilience. He is actively involved in executive development in a wide range of industries including financial services, food, energy and manufacturing. He also facilitates strategy workshops for top management teams and offers advisory services to senior executives. Venzin is a frequent speaker at corporate and industry events on such topics as company resilience, internationalization strategies, strategic decision-making dynamics, global knowledge-management systems, and the development of formal planning and control processes in large multinational firms. He is co-author of the book *Resilience* (2014).

Resilient Organizations

Responsible Leadership in Times of Uncertainty

**GUIA BEATRICE PIROTTI
AND MARKUS VENZIN**

CAMBRIDGE
UNIVERSITY PRESS

CAMBRIDGE
UNIVERSITY PRESS

University Printing House, Cambridge CB2 8BS, United Kingdom

One Liberty Plaza, 20th Floor, New York, NY 10006, USA

477 Williamstown Road, Port Melbourne, VIC 3207, Australia

4843/24, 2nd Floor, Ansari Road, Daryaganj, Delhi – 110002, India

79 Anson Road, #06–04/06, Singapore 079906

Cambridge University Press is part of the University of Cambridge.

It furthers the University's mission by disseminating knowledge in the pursuit of education, learning and research at the highest international levels of excellence.

www.cambridge.org
Information on this title: www.cambridge.org/9781107164666
DOI: 10.1017/9781316691151

First published 2017

Printed in the United Kingdom by Clays, St Ives plc

A catalogue record for this publication is available from the British Library

Library of Congress Cataloging-in-Publication Data
Names: Pirotti, Guia Beatrice, author. | Venzin, Markus, author.
Titles: Resilient organizations : responsible leadership in times of uncertainty / Guia Beatrice Pirotti and Markus Venzin.
Description: Cambridge, United Kingdom : Cambridge University Press, 2017. | Includes index.
Identifiers: LCCN 2016029181 | ISBN 9781107164666 (hardback) | ISBN 9781316616482 (paperback)
Subjects: LCSH: Strategic planning. | Business planning. | Organizational change. | Organizational effectiveness.
Classification: LCC HD30.28 .P524 2017 | DDC 658.4/012–dc23
LC record available at https://lccn.loc.gov/2016029181

ISBN 978-1-107-16466-6 Hardback
ISBN 978-1-316-61648-2 Paperback

Contents

Figures

Tables

Boxes

Introduction

Are you satisfied with how things are going in society, politics and business? In 2015, the Edelman Trust Barometer,[1] an instrument that measures confidence in institutions, governments and businesses, reached an all-time low among the informed public, indicating that leaders must change course. In general, leaders seem to have learned little from the financial crisis of 2008, which has been described as the result of 'a perfect storm of events':[2] excessive financial leverage, imprudent acquisitions, diversification based on dubious synergies, fallacious risk management and governance systems, and problems associated with the vertical and horizontal coordination of the banking network. On an economic level, the effects have been felt across the globe. In Europe, the sovereign-debt crisis created high levels of debt for families as well as trade deficits, while unemployment rose to a historical high and strict austerity measures had to be imposed. In the financial sector, many banks lost more than 90 per cent of their share prices. Many of those that survived have yet to recover. Was the financial-services crisis a rare event or are we likely to see more of such volatility in the future? How can firms prepare for such events? How can leaders change the way they make decisions?

This book is about resilience – the ability of companies to adapt to, resist and recover from external shocks. It is also about the role that leaders play in creating resilient firms. Like the sovereign-debt crisis, the financial crisis has shown that companies need more resilient business models. However, the goal of developing resilience – prospering despite catastrophic events – generally only appears to become a management priority after a shock has occurred. This is a little like doing the physiotherapy exercises a doctor prescribed long ago after yet another bout of back pain. How long should one do the exercises? Most likely until the pain passes and the physiotherapist is no longer checking.

[1] The Edelman Trust Barometer is available at: www.edelman.com.
[2] http://useconomy.about.com/od/Financial-Crisis.

A root cause of such behaviour is our inability to think about the long-term effects of our actions or to make decisions that maximize value creation for all stakeholders. Many leaders seem to have already forgotten the causes and effects of the 2008 crisis. They are happy to start each new fiscal year with the goal of meeting the expectations of their investors for the following four quarters.

To protect them from high expectations in the short term, new CEOs often begin their terms by issuing a 'shock profit warning', as was recently the case for Shell. Just two weeks after taking office in December 2013, Shell's new CEO, Ben van Beurden, announced that the company's profit would be 25 per cent lower in 2013 than it was in 2012. One year after their appointments, top executives usually explain that the results of their long-term measures are not yet observable. In the third year, many seem to be tempted to optimize annual profitability by gambling on risky projects, and by decreasing investments in marketing, R & D and other measures that may be advantageous to potential successors, while they prepare for the next mandate. CEOs of large American companies serve an average tenure of less than seven years (estimation for the period 1992–2005; Kaplan and Minton, 2012). These dynamics relate to many companies. However, we would like to see more CEOs who choose to restrain current performance in favour of their successors. Such generous conduct tends to be more evident in family businesses or in companies led by responsible leaders.

To support managers in their attempts to create resilient companies, we must start a debate on what constitutes responsible leadership and how it can be achieved. Responsible leaders maintain their personal and professional integrity. Moreover, they know how to build trust and ensure that certain ethical principles are respected. In more practical terms, responsible leaders follow business practices based on the dictates of sustainability and long-term development. In other words, they engage in 'sound and prudent management'. Such brave managers relinquish short-term profit in favour of stable and enduring long-term performance.

This book is for those managers and entrepreneurs who want to begin a journey aimed at increasing the resilience of their companies and, thereby, act as responsible leaders. In addition to evidence from international firms, the book features many examples from Italian firms that have excelled despite very difficult home-country conditions. We provide a method of measuring performance – VOLARE – that integrates existing measures with theoretical insights. We also offer concrete examples of seven drivers of resilience. In beginning our discussion of how to increase company resilience, we assert that:

1   Resilient companies show higher levels of authenticity. They approach the business in coherence with their traditions, competences, brand image and values.

2   Resilient companies have a high level of customer centricity. They are dedicated to the care of their customers and their needs, and they are willing to sacrifice short-term profitability in order to tie in customers in the long term. Employees identify with this strategy and are proud to be able to add value for customers before they think about shareholders.

3   Resilient companies have relatively simple business models and are determined to preserve key competencies by clearly linking their products and services to specific resources and capabilities.

4   Contrary to common beliefs, aggressive geographical diversification often increases the fragility of an organization, as it is difficult to assess and control all local risks. These problems increase with greater geographic diversification. Resilient companies hold a strong position in their home markets and prefer to develop strong positions in a few additional markets as opposed to weak positions in many markets.

5   Decision makers in resilient companies employ a long-term perspective that goes beyond their mandate.

6   Leaders in resilient companies make strategic decisions. In addition, they manage to combine speed with quality of decisions.

7   Resilient companies are led by CEOs and relatively small top-management teams (TMTs). Members of such teams have strong specialist and functional backgrounds, and they are bound by shared values.

This book will enable readers to analyse the merits of each of these assertions and assess their relevance for their own contexts. In particular, in today's business world, managers find themselves having to make decisions in a wide variety of areas. For example, they need to understand how to internationalize and in which markets; which businesses are worthy of investments; whether to lean towards intense diversification of activities or focus on a specific business; which image to convey to consumers; how to motivate employees; whether to simplify the organizational structure; and whether to make decisions quickly or to be meticulous at the expense of speed. An understanding of how to act in the face of these trade-offs can ensure survival beyond a crisis, thereby creating the possibility to be resilient. The book serves as an intuitive guide to facing these challenges and to achieving sustainable results over time.

We trust that this book will help trigger not only a shift that puts business processes on a path towards greater resilience, but also a change towards responsible leadership. We need leaders who think about the consequences of their actions and take responsibility for them. As simple as this may sound, it requires fundamental change, which is not easy to achieve. We often encounter managers who are disappointed or disheartened, and who find it difficult to change things around them. In the face of the challenges posed by energy overconsumption, waste proliferation and population growth, it is difficult to establish new standards and to change behaviours. Managers may find themselves thinking: 'What can I do as a small player in this game? If I change, the system will not be affected at all.' Such thoughts, although understandable, frequently end up in a finger-pointing exercise of identifying someone who starts changing. When you feel unmotivated or like giving up, we recommend watching a short video in which Malala Yousafzai,[3] a fourteen-year-old girl and a recipient of the Nobel Peace Prize, recounts her battle to ensure the right to education of women in her country. We all need a little of her energy to make changes for the better.

This book is based on a research project entitled 'The Nature of Resilient Firms' carried out at SDA Bocconi School of Management. The three-year study had the dual objective of measuring resilience and ascertaining its main drivers, and of identifying the international 'champions' in economic sectors that were particularly affected by external shocks. These companies managed to produce positive results despite the crisis. The project also identified those companies that experienced greater problems. The VOLARE indicator, which is described later in this book, enabled us to assign a resilience rating from 0 to 10 (with 0 being the lowest and 10 the highest) to 705 listed companies active in seven industries. These industries included banking, automotive, pharmaceutical and energy, all of which have been affected recently by external shocks. We analysed the main choices implemented by these companies, and we combined quantitative and qualitative research techniques in order to determine the drivers of resilience. The information obtained was integrated with secondary data, such as business documents, institutional sites and newspaper articles.

The book is organized in ten chapters. The first chapter offers a brief overview of the meanings and applications of the term 'resilience' in the fields of psychology, ecology, systems, materials science and economics. These different

---

[3] The video is available on YouTube at: www.youtube.com/watch?v=gjGL6YY6oMs.

spheres provide conceptual cues that allow us to develop our definition of re-silience as the ability of companies to anticipate shocks and not bend to them. We also explain the underlying model of our research – resilient businesses show relatively high and stable performance over time. Such companies have learned to manage some strategic variables or drivers of resilience better than others.

In the second chapter, we explain that the first step towards resilience lies in changing the way that we measure performance. After a brief discussion of the limitations of commonly used performance indicators, we introduce a new method for measuring long-term financial results. The proposed indi-cator is called VOLARE, and it is a formal performance-appraisal system that combines the average long-term (ten years) return on equity and the volatility of return on equity. The application of this performance measure to a large set of companies from different industries allows us to distinguish resilient firms from firms that are less able to absorb market shocks. We also propose us-ing VOLARE when making investment decisions on the firm or business-unit level. Too often, firms only look at short-term profitability measures when allocating resources to business units. As a result, they underestimate the long-term profitability impact as well as the risks associated with such investments.

The following chapters describe the individual resilience drivers in detail. Chapter 3 sets out to improve our understanding of the role of authenticity – the ability to be credible in the eyes of consumers and shareholders. We de-fine authenticity and how it applies to business-management practices. There are two types of authenticity. The first is 'type authenticity': the more one is identifiable with a specific category (e.g. type of product, market, customer segment) the more authentic one is. The second is 'moral authenticity': the more one is identifiable with some predetermined reference values, the greater one's authenticity. Authentic companies are recognizable and credible to con-sumers, employees and social actors. As a result, authenticity has a positive effect on resilience. It serves as the underlying logic for understanding all of the decision challenges and drivers of resilience described in the subsequent chapters.

Chapter 4 discusses customer centricity – the ability to prioritize the customer above any other stakeholder – and suggests three ways in which it can be pursued: love for the product, excellent processes and innovation. Companies that know how to develop customer centricity tend to be more resilient than companies that try to please their shareholders first.

Chapter 5 explores the 'ideal' level of product diversification. The relationship between diversification and performance has been studied for some time and has given rise to ambiguous interpretations. Our research shows that when a company focuses on a few products, the likelihood of being resilient and obtaining a high VOLARE rating increases. Most turnaround processes start with a return to the core business, which implies divestment of superfluous elements, and focusing on primary and core competencies. The rules for pursuing a product-focused strategy are therefore outlined with the use of examples and best practices.

Chapter 6 introduces the resilience driver 'market focus'. In this regard, we discuss the criteria for selecting geographical markets in which to operate. In the internationalization process, caution offers rewards in terms of resilience. Size is no guarantee for stable and positive performance over time, especially in the presence of external shocks. Resilient companies selectively invest in foreign markets and develop a set of coherent geographical areas as a competitive base. They develop foreign markets with the objective of making them second-home markets – markets in which they are as strong as in their home market. Resilient firms prefer to obtain their foreign revenues from a strong presence in five markets rather than from a weak presence in fifty.

Chapter 7 identifies long-term orientation as a key variable in the level of business resilience. Too often, decisions only take short-term results and current profit maximization into account. In contrast, strategic decisions are complex decisions that commit substantial amounts of resources to the purpose of achieving a desired long-term vision. These decisions are hard to reverse and often reduce short-term profitability. Companies must therefore possess a type of ambidexterity – the ability to manage current activities while developing strategic activities or projects. Concern about the results of potential successors – and acting accordingly – increases the likelihood of being resilient. The chapter explores the nature of strategic projects, the origins of a long-term orientation and how this capacity can be developed.

Chapter 8 examines the ability of TMTs to make strategic decisions. Due to the increasing complexity of the economic environment, companies desiring good and stable performance over time must be able to make decisions faster and faster without sacrificing quality. A well-designed formal strategic process enables companies to be efficient in decision making and thereby save time, and to gather ideas from people within and outside the organization, and articulate their contributions. The decision-making process can occur in unstructured and informal meetings, but it can also be organized within strategic workshops or annual events programmed to define the strategic guidelines. Knowledge of how to organize a strategic workshop helps improve the quality of decisions. This chapter proposes a strategic-process tool and describes how to best organize a strategic workshop.

Chapter 9 explores the last driver of our resilience model: ownership structure, top-management-team composition and organizational design decisions that have an impact on effectiveness. We start with a discussion of the ownership structure's impact on the composition of TMTs. We then discuss the optimal size for TMTs, and whether their members should be specialists or generalists.

Finally, we conclude by providing a practical process tool for managers and entrepreneurs who wish to increase the resilience of their organizations. As firms are not naturally resilient, they have to be made resilient. Our resilience model identifies seven core drivers of resilience that support the process of making a firm more resilient. In the final section, we show managers how to test the level of resilience in their companies using a benchmark score.

CHAPTER 1

Investing in the Ability to Withstand Shocks

The 2013 World Economic Forum in Davos was entitled 'Resilient Dynamism'. The event description read, 'This new leadership context requires successful organisations to master strategic agility and to build risk resilience.' According to the Forum's report *Building National Resilience to Global Risks*, resilience allows organizations to survive and thrive in an increasingly interdependent and hyper-connected world. Resilient companies work to recover as quickly as possible after environmental or economic failures. Resilience has become a call to action – a call for change – in a world that has gone through crises and unexpected events. However, what does this term, which is spreading among economists, sociologists, ecologists and psychologists, actually mean?

The term *resilience* derives from the Latin *resalio*, the frequentative of the verb *salio*, which means 'bounce'. In one of its original meanings, it refers to getting back on a capsized boat. The term found its first applications in physics and mechanics, where it is used to measure the impact resistance of a material, and a material's ability to regain its original shape after being deformed, flattened, elongated or subjected to any change. Resilience has traditionally been linked to engineering studies, especially to metallurgy, where it indicates the ability of a metal to resist the impulsive forces applied to it. This concept can also be applied to the dynamics of liquids, in which case it expresses the capacity of a system to return to a state of equilibrium following a disturbance and the time it takes to do so. A classic example used to explain resilience is that of a pebble in a pond. The pebble is thrown into the water, creating concentric circles until the water returns to the initial stasis and the circles disappear. Another example is a metal called nitinol, which is a shape-memory alloy (i.e. a metal that remembers its original shape) that, even when deformed, can return to its original shape after being heated.

In computing, resilience refers to the ability of a system to continue operating properly despite faults in one or more elements. System resilience indicates tolerance to failures, faults and breakdowns. In anthropology, the concept is discussed in terms of societies, ethnicities, languages and belief systems that provide evidence of resilience. In chemistry and biology, resilience is defined as homeostasis – the ability of a system or organism to return to its starting conditions or to maintain its initial functions in a dynamic, changing environment where a large number of interacting forces must be maintained in a more or less unstable equilibrium.

In order to develop a complete picture of resilience and to outline the nature of its drivers, we offer a brief overview of selected academic areas in which resilience has been implemented. Each area serves as a basis for drawing similarities and differences with respect to our definition.

IN PSYCHOLOGY

In psychology, resilience refers to the ability to positively face traumatic events and to positively reorganize our lives when confronted with difficulties. It is the ability to rebuild oneself while remaining receptive to the positive opportunities that life offers. Resilient people are those who manage to survive highly adverse situations.

The term was first used in 1982 by the American psychologist Emmy Werner in a longitudinal study of unschooled children of the Hawaiian islands entitled *Vulnerable but Invincible: A Longitudinal Study of Resilient Children and Youth* (Werner, 1982). These children were without family, and they had been exposed to violence and disease. The study showed that only 30 per cent of these children were literate, had work and had created families. In terms of classic psychology, about one-third of these infants had all of the prerequisites for a prognosis of mental or social disadvantage, as they were exposed to numerous risk factors, including difficult births, poverty, families with alcohol problems, mental illness and aggression. However, in contrast to likely expectations, one-third of these children – seventy-two to be exact – succeeded in improving their living conditions in adulthood. They became adults capable of initiating stable relations, undertaking work and doing their utmost for others. This discovery of the possibility for improvement opened up a field of study on those protective factors that can promote proper development. Among these factors are personal characteristics (e.g. resilient children have temperamental characteristics that provoke positive responses from family members and strangers, pronounced autonomy, a strong social orientation and an optimistic view of their experiences); supportive parents; a strong bond with nonparent caretakers (such as aunts or teachers); and involvement in a community (such as church or a group like the YMCA).

In 2007, Pietro Trabucchi, a sport psychologist, wrote the book *I Resist, Therefore I Am* in which he proposed that the majority of people tend to be resilient. In fact, people are able to adapt to and learn to overcome even the most severe adversity. Trabucchi writes,

> It seems that in recent years the usual perspective has reversed a little: resilience is the norm in humans, not fragility. In World War II, London was extensively bombed. Serious repercussions were feared on the psychic equilibrium of inhabitants. The opposite happened. Admissions to psychiatric wards decreased, as did suicides. The same thing happened in the acute stages of the war for the independence of Northern Ireland, and during the race riots in the United States in the 60s and 70s.
>
> (Trabucchi, 2007)

We all are naturally resilient because we are, in general, characterized by an 'optimism bias' (Sharot, 2012). In other words, we tend to overestimate positive events and underestimate negative events. Our approach to divorce serves as an example. Statistics suggest that the probability of divorce is around 40 per cent. However, two people who marry tend to estimate the probability of leaving each other over the years at 0 per cent. If they happen to divorce, the card they can play is to marry a second time.

Optimistic people seem to be naturally more resilient than others. A study conducted on a sample of students in the early months of 2001 and in the months following the September 11, 2001, terrorist attacks confirms that resilience is associated with life satisfaction, optimism and tranquillity. The study showed that people with more resilience had better moods and, after the attacks, they reported more positive emotions than their peers with lower resilience values. The same study also provides evidence that the ability to develop one's own resources after a critical event – the ability to be resilient – is mediated by experiencing positive emotions (Fredrickson, Tugade, Waugh and Larkin, 2003).

Personal resilience has often been investigated in the military. Seligman (2011) studied positive psychology. In 2008 he met General George W. Casey Jr, commander of the Multi-National Force in Iraq. The General asked Seligman how his field of study applied to military life, and Seligman responded by arguing that the reaction of individuals to adversity is normally distributed. On the one end of the spectrum are soldiers who fall into depression or resort to suicide following trauma and war. In the middle are the majority of soldiers, who initially become depressed or face anxiety, but return to form after a month or two. In other words, they continue from the point where they were before the trauma. On the other end of the spectrum are soldiers who show post-traumatic growth. They experience shock, but have the strength to eventually feel better than before the traumatic event. These are the people that Friedrich Nietzsche defines with 'what does not kill me, makes me stronger'.

Psychology studies have also been applied to enterprises. Resilient companies are made up of resilient people. Dean Becker, president and CEO of Adaptive Learning Systems, says, 'More than education, more than experience, more than training, a person's level of resilience will determine who succeeds and who fails. That's true in the cancer ward, it's true in the Olympics, and it's true in the boardroom' (Coutu, 2002, p. 22).

In our research we took two cues from these psychology studies. First, the same principle that applies to people can be applied to companies – the drivers that determine whether a company will be successful in the face of external shocks can be identified. Second, shocks should be used to make firms stronger, a little like soldiers who become stronger after a trauma.

IN ECOLOGY

The ecological concept of resilience was introduced by Crawford Holling in the early 1970s. Holling (1973) used it to define the ability of natural systems or social-ecological systems (i.e. integrated human and ecological systems) to absorb disturbances and reorganize during a change while essentially maintaining the same functions and the same equilibrium. A system has the ability to evolve in multiple states that are different from the states prior to the disorder, thereby maintaining the vitality of its functions and structures. In other words, a forest has the ability to regenerate and even to live with an element of natural or human disorder if that disorder is not definitive deforestation. For example, in the Amazon rainforest the problem is the expansion of the agricultural frontier through the construction of new roads. Resilience depends on society's capacity to cohabitate with the ecosystem without destroying it.

Andrew Zolli and Ann Marie Healy's book (2011) *Resilience: Why Things Bounce Back* (Zolli and Healy, 2012) contributes to the debate in this field. Zolli runs PopTech, a network of innovators in the field of technology. In the face of the great challenges of our time – social inequalities, pollution and climate change – Zolli argues that the 'sustainability' buzzword is proving inadequate. He highlights that talking about sustainability implies a goal of restoring perfect balance, while it is much more realistic to learn to manage a world in perpetual imbalance.

An interesting reflection on resilience cited in the book concerns the city of New York after it was ravaged by Hurricane Sandy in 2012. Although the trauma of the hurricane had not yet come to an end and the damage had not yet been fully absorbed, the city decided to reflect on how a large metropolis could prepare for extreme weather events. The debate considered both the possibility of facing disasters and the possibility of adapting to them. The first approach would require investing in the construction of robust physical barriers – expensive but still vulnerable dams – to protect the city from future tsunamis. The second approach considered the solutions developed by nature itself, which were far more flexible and less expensive. Such solutions included the exploitation of wetland areas (such as marshes, natural swamps, lakes and ponds) as moving barriers to block an unexpected influx of water and lessen its destructive capacity.

In 2004 a group of economists began to study the resilience of small nations. In a paper entitled *Economic Vulnerability and Resilience Concepts and Measurements* (2008), a group of researchers led by Lino Briguglio explain the concepts of vulnerability (i.e. potential exposure to external shocks) and resilience (i.e. the ability to react to those shocks with appropriate policies and actions) (Briguglio et al., 2008). They explain the concepts using the example of Singapore. Due to its small size, Singapore is more comparable to a city-state than to a nation. Its limited geographic scope makes it highly vulnerable. It is dependent on exports and basically helpless in the face of external shocks deriving from the global economy. Nevertheless, Singapore has become a laboratory of resilience, as it has been able to implement the principles of good governance and social development. Resilience is actionable in any country and only requires adoption of effective laws and rules.

The analysis of resilience in ecology suggests that the need to deal with a challenge and to establish the rules of survival derive from the external environment, which is characterized by 'constant volatility' or the 'new normal'. In fact, in a world in perpetual imbalance, investments in resilience are required, as is responsible leadership. If the forest is in grave danger, managers should try to be the tree that is not felled.

In our research, we took two cues from these ecology studies. First, firms that are stressed and exposed to external shocks can survive and prosper by establishing some rules of conduct. Second, size does not necessarily offer good protection against shocks.

IN SYSTEMS

In systems, resilience is the ability to remain within certain limits or to maintain balance despite fluctuations caused by external forces. It refers to the ability to cushion external attacks and, as such, becomes a necessary feature of any kind of system. For example, lakes with an alkaline-buffer system were able to resist the acidification caused by acid rain in the 1980s, while more sensitive lakes with less alkaline in southern Sweden acidified and became devoid of higher life forms.

The resilience of social systems refers to the processes that take place within a social environment affected by a traumatic event. These processes are intended to support and rebuild social bonds and a sense of belonging.

In computer systems, the term 'resilience' indicates the ability to adapt to the conditions of use and to resist wear, and thereby ensure continued provision of services. These goals can be achieved by means of redundancy techniques. For example, if a computer is a few years old and has been used a great deal, frequent back-ups are advisable. Resilience can be enhanced by duplicating the available resource in order to reduce the risk of a breakdown or a loss of data.

In engineering systems, resilience is defined as the flexural strength/shock resistance of a material. The Charpy test consists of dropping a pendulum of known mass and length from a known height towards a material that is positioned on two supports. The results of that test gives the energy absorbed during the drop. In this case, resilience is equal to the energy absorbed per surface unit.

In industrial-relations systems, supply and demand are created, knowledge of products or semi-finished products in the production process is transferred and relations are established among competitors or other social actors. These exchanges and relations make the environment very unpredictable and uncertain. For this reason, mathematical or quantitative models are used to study the resilience of the industrial system – the system's ability to withstand shocks.

In all of these systems, resilience requires two elements: (1) an ability to recognize risk factors on every systemic level (e.g. individual, family, community, society) and to predict subsequent problems for an individual within the system or for the system itself; and (2) the subsequent adaptation of the system if necessary.

IN FIRMS

The resilience of individuals or materials can easily be measured using appropriate tests. Consider the tests that the US Navy SEALs must take to gain access to training. That training, if passed successfully, leads to their recruitment. The tests listed below must be carried out in sequence with a maximum break of three minutes between each. The values are the minimums that must be met to be considered eligible for training:

★ swimming 500 yards (about 455 m) in less than 12 minutes and 30 seconds,
★ forty-two push-ups in 2 minutes,
★ fifty sit-ups in 2 minutes,
★ six pull-ups (from a lying position), and
★ a 1.5-mile run (about 2.4 km) wearing boots and long trousers in less than 11 minutes and 30 seconds.[1]

Such a test allows the resilience of an individual to be identified and subsequently enhanced. However, at the firm level, observing and measuring resilience seems more difficult. In this context, resilience refers to an organization's ability to continue to operate and remain efficient in the face of negative external events. A firm is resilient if it is able to ensure stable performance over time despite the turmoil and difficulties of the environment.

To improve our understanding we can examine cases of failure or bankruptcy. In 1992, for example, Hoover launched a marketing campaign to boost sales. The UK division of Hoover had a large stock of unsold washing machines and other appliances. To free up warehouses it promised free airline tickets to customers who purchased products worth more than GBP 100. However, Hoover failed to foresee the large number of requests that would result from this campaign. People purchased appliances not necessarily because they needed them but because they were interested in the tickets. Initially, the offer included two round-trip tickets to a European destination of the customer's choice. When it was extended to include routes to the United States, the damage was immense given that the price of an intercontinental flight far exceeded GBP 100 worth of products. Hoover suffered heavy losses.

Due to the events of September 11, Swissair did not have the money to pay for fuel and kept all of its aircraft on the ground in October 2001. About 39,000 passengers were stranded at various airports around the world. The damage to the company's image was immense. The company's policy of undertaking unlimited mergers and acquisitions financed with debt had caused its collapse. In 2005, after setting aside national pride, Swissair was sold to Germany's Lufthansa, which helped it to become a profit-maker over time.

Some firms manage to use a crisis to gain competitiveness. In his book *Reorganize for Resilience*, Ranjay Gulati (2010) studies the most recent crises

---

[1] See Official Naval Special Warfare website: www.sealswcc.com.

that hit the global economy. He estimates the survival rate of companies at 60 per cent. In such situations a large proportion of companies focus exclusively on survival and reduce costs as much as possible in order to re-emerge when the storm has passed. A smaller group (5–10% of survivors) uses a crisis as a time of development with respect to competitors. Walmart, the US retail giant, is an example of the latter. This multinational managed to extend its outlets throughout the United States, particularly when the crisis had devastated many small traders who could not compete with the power of Walmart due to their small size.

Many Korean and Chinese companies have found new opportunities thanks to the recent financial crisis. For the Korean giant Samsung, 2012 was the year in which it conquered the summit. In Q1 2012, with nearly 100 million units sold, it surpassed global leader Nokia's sales of 82 million units to become the world's leading producer of mobile phones. In addition, it surpassed Apple, which continues to pursue legal battles against Samsung regarding patents, flexible chips and displays. In 2015, Samsung's market share stood at more than 25 per cent, which can be compared to Nokia's 22 per cent and Apple's 9.5 per cent. In hindsight, Samsung had already won the smartphone battle by late 2011 in terms of scale, as its product line had been consolidated thanks to the international success of Galaxy products.

Similarly, at the end of 2010, Haier – a Chinese company that became the world leader in household appliances in less than thirty years – had increased sales of its appliances by 23 per cent, and lifted its turnover by 38 per cent in the Americas, 32 per cent in Europe and 13 per cent in Asia. In 2011, it announced net sales of USD 23.3 billion, an increase of 12 per cent relative to the previous year. The brand became increasingly global. In 2004, Haier decided to invest in Italy. Despite the crisis, the favourable tide reached Europe. In 2012, turnover in the Italian market increased by 25 per cent compared to 2011 (Planet Tech, 12 September 2012)[2]. Enrico Ligabue, managing director of Haier Italy and Greece, said:

> Maybe our good luck is that we cannot compete with the household appliance giants in terms of technology, resources or investments. Perhaps it is easier. Big companies that have an extremely large market share are the first to suffer. We compete with small local producers. In these situations, brands emerge that have something different to say, such

[2] See 'A Milano la strategia 2013 di Haier Italia' at: www.e-duesse.it/News/Cons.-Electronics/A-Milano-la-strategia-2013-di-Haier-Italia-149476.

as Haier. The value for money that we offer meets the demands of the medium-low customer segment, today turning more and more towards the medium range. The goal is to sell products that are in line with the market, therefore a medium line, without however relinquishing good quality. It was the right offer at the right time. We try to understand the needs of our customers and have invested in brand awareness. Up to 2010, we did not have many resources to give the brand visibility. In 2011, the choice in Italy was to invest in communications. It was a turning point.

(Pirotti, 2013)

For both companies, the crisis represented an opportunity, as it created market turbulence and a shift in customer needs. Samsung was able to offer high-tech products at lower prices, thereby meeting the needs of a new market segment composed of customers who were no longer willing to pay premium prices. Samsung's success was also made possible by its size and its ability to reap profit from economies of scale. Similarly, Haier managed to address the medium-low-end customer segment, which was growing rapidly due to the ongoing economic crisis.

As these examples illustrate, a crisis creates volatility and has the potential to redistribute market shares. However, resilience is more than the ability to adapt, move and innovate. It also encompasses an ability to return to a state of efficiency and effectiveness after the equilibrium of the business system has been disturbed. To do so, a firm must be able to read external feedback, show some flexibility, and transfer the knowledge and resources needed to overcome the trigger event. In 2000, Barnett and Pratt (Barnett and Pratt, 2000) theorized that the primary emphasis of an organization should not be on rigid or bureaucratic responses – when a firm adopts a rigid stance towards necessary changes, the chances of survival and development decrease. Weick and Sutcliffe (2007) argue that 'the essence of resilience is therefore the intrinsic ability of an organisation (system) to maintain or regain a dynamically stable state, which allows it to continue operations after a major mishap and/or in the presence of continuous stress'.

In sum, two perspectives are offered by organizational literature. The first views resilience as the ability to cope with adverse situations, and knowing how to recover when those situations have passed or changed (Balu, 2001; Gittell, Cameron, Lim and Rivas, 2006; Rudolph and Repenning, 2002; Sutcliffe and Vogus, 2003). The second relates not only to adaptation but also to the ability to develop new skills and create new opportunities when dealing with a crisis (Freeman, Hirschhorn and Maltz, 2004; Jamrog et al., 2006;

Lengnick-Hall, Beck and Lengnick-Hall, 2011). The most comprehensive definition of resilience is one that integrates the two perspectives. Resilient companies: (1) know how to absorb an adverse situation by developing awareness
of what is happening and reflecting on how much has to be done; and (2)
develop specific responses and adaptive-transformation activities that enable
long-term survival (Lengnick-Hall, Beck and Lengnick-Hall, 2011).

OUR DEFINITION OF RESILIENCE

Muhammad Ali is known for his statement, 'nside of a ring or out, ain't nothing wrong with going down. It's staying down that's wrong.' The uncertainty of
economic competition has been compared to the uncertainty in a boxing ring
(Sull, 2009). Prior to a match, a boxer can study the moves that his opponent
used in the past, but he cannot precisely predict what will happen during the
match in terms of which punches will be used, in what sequence and with how
much force. The two contenders may have very different approaches during
the match. Some boxers, such as Jack Johnson, have great agility. Johnson was
the first African American world heavyweight boxing champion (1908–15).
He was sprightly and quick to avoid the opponent's blows, but also ready to
launch fast and frequent attacks. Conversely, some boxers have great physical
strength, such as George Foreman, and formulate their tactics to absorb many
punches and punch when the opponent shows signs of fatigue. Of course, true
champions manage to combine agility with the capacity to absorb hits.

Like boxing champions, firms need to have systems that allow them to
avoid shocks and systems that allow them to absorb the shocks which they
cannot avoid. Three elements of resilience can be identified from this boxing
metaphor:

1 *Robustness*. Similar to a tree that withstands the storm, companies do not
   bend and are able to absorb shocks.
2 *Recovery*. Companies bend in the face of external shocks, but they know
   how to get back up.
3 *Resourcefulness*. Companies bend and change position.

Robustness

Certain people are called 'prophets of doom'. They are preparing for the
end of the world. When it comes, they will be ready to deal with it with the
resources they have amassed. This is the case for Lonny Sundvall, who follows

a curious ritual every morning. 'The first thing I do when I get up: check the US Geological Survey website for earthquakes and volcanoes. Then I check the observatories. Then I check the space weather', reveals Sundvall, who lives in Oregon (Huffington Post, 2011)[3]. Sundvall is neither a seismologist nor a volcanologist. His hometown, Roseburg, is not located on a major fault line nor near a volcano. Sundvall is forty-nine years old, he works in a warehouse and he belongs to the growing community of people who pay a great deal of attention to news of disasters in the world. Like other prophets of doom, Sundvall has a bunker to be used in case of emergency and he accumulates canned provisions, which would be useful if the apocalypse becomes a reality. In his own way, Lonny Sundvall is robust – should there be any large-scale natural disasters, he will probably survive using the means with which he has equipped himself.

Some companies specialize in the construction of underground buildings or bunkers to withstand the dangers of nuclear, biological, chemical and seismic activities. One of the most important companies active in this line of work in the United States is Hardened Structures. Its operating method is based on an analysis of the possible risks. It designs buildings according to customer needs and constructs them using more durable materials in absolute terms than the nature of the risk the customers think they may face. In fact, the underground real-estate market has become a veritable industry that continues to expand. A feature that sets it apart from other areas is the level of secrecy with which bunkers can be built. Those who commission this type of building usually do not want their neighbours to know what they are building. In recent years, the business has substantially grown in the United States. People seem to show an increasingly higher level of preparation to handle disasters.

In corporate terms, BMW or Audi can be described as examples of robustness. When faced with the recent crisis, they were able to maintain good results without having to implement major changes. The alignment among their selected targets, the products offered and their organizational structures worked prior to and during the crisis. In other words, the strategic choices these two German automakers had made allowed them to withstand the challenge without bending. Their continuous investments in technology and design allowed the two producers to meet the needs of a traditional, sophisticated, skilled market segment willing to pay a higher price for product quality, design and durability.

---

[3] See 'Mayan prophecy 2012 catastrophe' at: www.huffingtonpost.com/2011/12/14/mayan-prophecy-2012-catastrophe_n_1146092.html#s277466&title=1999_2012_3797.

However, for Audi, which is part of the Volkswagen Group, we include a disclaimer regarding the predictive value of our research. The analysis presented above focuses on business performance during a specific period of time (i.e. 2001–2010). Throughout that period, several strategic and organizational factors enabled both Audi and BMW to successfully resist external shocks. While we are confident that the seven resilience drivers presented in this book generally help firms overcome external shocks, we do not claim to be able to draw conclusions about Volkswagen's ability to mitigate the effects of the recent scandal concerning the manipulation of emissions data.

Recovery

An excellent example of the recovery element of resilience is found in the recovery of the internationally recognized pianist, composer and conductor Giovanni Allevi. Allevi holds an honours degree in philosophy, as well as two Conservatory diplomas awarded with full honours in piano and composition. His songs define the tenets of new 'contemporary classical music' through language that seeks to unite the sanctity of traditional classical music with modern tastes. Due to his intellectual commitment, Allevi has not only been met with an enthusiastic audience, but he has also received acknowledgement and appreciation from Italian President Giorgio Napolitano, Pope Benedict XVI and Nobel laureate Mikhail Gorbachev. Nevertheless, he has also been subject to harsh criticism, which sent him into a lengthy depression. It all began in 2008 when the violinist Uto Ughi attacked him in an interview, saying he was 'offended by Allevi's success' (*La Stampa*, 24 December 2008).[4] For two years, the pianist disappeared from the scene. However, thanks to his 'love for music and a profound acceptance of what happened' (*La Stampa*, 24 December 2008), he finally found his own way of reacting – he composed *Sunrise*, a concerto for piano and orchestra, and violin and orchestra that broke box-office records in terms of a completely sold-out tour and the number of CDs sold.

The reaction mechanism is similar for companies. Following the death of its founder in 2001, the Korean automaker Hyundai had to divest many of its businesses and faced a serious setback. Yet, by analysing the quality-focused strategy established from 2001 to 2011, Hyundai was eventually able to present itself as one of the most solid and promising companies in the auto sector. The company's reaction to the difficult time was to the fullest, which

---

[4] The interview 'Il successo di Allevi? Mi offende' is available at: www.lastampa.it/2008/12/24/spettacoli/il-successo-di-allevi-mi-offende-JPzmyr6NI0F4RbEMGfKXsM/pagina.html.

meant that it was able get back on its feet. The solution was a new focus on quality, which started with a marketing initiative. When faced with a huge drop in sales in 1998, Hyundai's desperate US executive leaders had launched a consumer-research project. They discovered a highly positive reaction to the prospect of a three-part warranty deal (ten-year/100,000-mile powertrain protection, five-year/60,000-mile bumper-to-bumper coverage and five-year/unlimited mileage roadside assistance). They proposed calling it 'America's Best Warranty'. The warranty represented a massive bet on the company's ability to improve. Without consistent quality improvements, the company would face a huge amount of claims and bad publicity. This programme ensured that Hyundai created internal commitment to massive change programmes aimed at quality improvements.

Resourcefulness

The third element involves a shift – a real transition from one sector to another or a substantial repositioning of activities. For example, some actors who have played key roles in certain films, such as James Caviezel who played Jesus in *The Passion of the Christ*, are subsequently unable to build a solid career in film and, in most cases, turn to television. Caviezel has since starred in the successful television series *The Prisoner*.

To cite an example from corporate life, Nokia seems to have an impressive capacity to reinvent its business model. The history of the Finnish company and its shifts from one business to another show that it has been able to reinvent itself and adapt as necessary to market needs. From cellulose to cell phones, the changes that Nokia has put in place are characterized by a high degree of agility. Nokia is the name of a river, near which the mining engineer Knut Fredrik Idestam built a sawmill in 1865 to exploit the current in order to process wood and cellulose. At the beginning of the twentieth century, a leader in the manufacturing of rubber boots was attracted by the energy produced by the river. The Finnish rubber company started using 'Nokia' as its trademark. Shortly after the First World War, the company, which at one point became the most important supplier of boots for the Finnish Army, acquired the nearby wood-processing mill. In 1922, the two companies entered into a holding agreement with the main national provider of cables for telephones and telegraphs. After the Second World War, the group's cable branch offered its services to the USSR as a supplier of the material that Finland had to provide under the peace treaty. In the 1970s, Nokia increased its commitment to the telecommunications industry by developing automated switching instruments. In 1977, Kari Kairamo became chairman. Kairamo had studied in the United States and did not share the pro-Soviet tradition typical of Finnish entrepreneurs. He instead targeted televisions and personal computers. His successor, Jorma Ollila, who became chairman in 1992, concentrated on the electronics industry by changing the product focus from computers to mobile phones while the latter's boom was still in its infancy. Nokia's cable division was sold. The decision to focus on the telecommunications industry and on the production of mobile phones paid off, turning Nokia into one of the most important companies in the world in these two sectors. Only time will tell whether the company will be able to utilize its abilities to again climb the leadership board now that it has been acquired by Microsoft for EUR 5.44 billion.

Apple offers another example. When Steve Jobs was appointed CEO ad interim in the late 1990s after having been sent away a few years earlier, Apple was on the verge of bankruptcy. Jobs worked hard, surveying every product team in the company. Each team had to convince him that its product was essential to the company's strategy. If the product was not profitable, it was usually removed from the product line. 'After two years as interim CEO, Steve Jobs completely turned Apple around. He restored the company's public image, implemented a successful and focused new strategy, attracted software developers, and launched highly innovative and awe-inspiring products on the marketplace. The confused product lines had turned into a simple yet powerful product matrix made by iMac, Power Mac, iBook and PowerBook'.[5] About fifteen years later – one year after Jobs' death – the company reached the highest level of capitalization in its history – USD 660 billion.[6]

Based on our discussion of these three elements, we define *resilience as the process by which firms make strategic decisions (drivers) that increase their robustness, recovery and resourcefulness, and thereby ensure stable and sustained superior performance over time*. The three main ingredients of resilience – robustness, recovery and resourcefulness – are related to many change-management models and theories, where 'change management' is defined as a structured approach to organizational change that makes it possible to switch from the current structure to a desired future structure. Change management encompasses such concepts as flexibility, willingness to change and organization's elasticity in facing new challenges. In extreme cases, firms engage in

---

[5] See 'The return to Apple' at: http://allaboutstevejobs.com/bio/longbio/longbio_08.php.
[6] See 'Steve Jobs: the return, 1997–2001' at: www.businessweek.com/magazine/the-return
-19972011-10062011.html.

turnaround-management exercises, which are defined as processes dedicated to the renewal of companies in a short period of time – in a crisis situation – through the use of analytical and planning tools. The aim of such exercises is to return to good financial results as quickly as possible. They involve an evaluation phase, in which the factors that have caused the crisis are identified; a recovery phase, in which extraordinary and urgent measures are taken to solve problems in the short term; and a restructuring phase, in which decisions are made for the long term (Barker and Duhaime, 1997). If the above steps are appropriately structured, the results in terms of performance should return to the positive.

We have seen many turnaround processes. One of the most recent is Qantas, Australia's national air carrier. In 2014, Qantas announced a severe cost-cutting programme and a corporate-restructuring programme aimed at returning the airline to profitability. CEO Alan Joyce unveiled a record USD 2.8 billion loss. Then, in February 2016, Joyce announced a record first-half underlying profit of $921 million, a 234 per cent surge in the six months to December, including net profit of $688 million.[7] However, while Qantas has proven able to bounce back from poor performance, we would not label Qantas a highly resilient firm. Organizations that show high resilience are able to avoid such drastic restructuring phases because they act before they find themselves at the brink of bankruptcy.

The following section anticipates the main results of our study – that resilient firms are able to achieve stable, positive performance in the long run. To do so, companies need to know or learn how to best manage seven strategic variables, or decisional trade-offs. While we do not claim that this list of factors that influence resiliency is exhaustive, we suggest that thinking about these variables and contextualizing their implications will have a positive impact on the firm's capacity to deliver sustained superior performance.

OUR MODEL OF RESILIENCE

Commonly used models to study resilience have two problems. First, resilience is only indirectly defined on the basis of its drivers and it is not directly intended to be an exogenous variable (i.e. performance objective). Second, many organizational features are incorporated into the concept of resilience, such as agility and absorption (Sull, 2009), or 'capture' and 'governance'

---

[7] See 'Qantas: The most remarkable turnaround in aviation history? at: www.icas.com/ca-today
  -news/qantas-nine-lives-flying-kangaroo.

strategies (Carmeli and Markman, 2011). Moreover, it is difficult to measure resilience prior to a negative event. An organization's latent resilience is composed of resources, strategies and capacities that are extremely difficult to measure. Consequently, we propose a model that limits itself to rigorously measuring the company's ability to absorb a shock and achieve good results in the long term (i.e. sustained superior performance, SSP) and is less specific regarding the issue of what drives the company's resilience. This implies a need to verify two conditions for companies to be defined as resilient: (1) the company must be exposed to an external event or a complex crisis; and (2) the company must show above-average performance before, during and after the crisis.

We measure SSP using an indicator called VOLARE, which we explain in detail in Chapter 2. It takes into account a relatively long period (ten years) and assigns values ranging from 0 (lowest) to 10 (highest) to 705 listed companies in seven different sectors affected by external shocks in recent years. The main focal industries are banking, automotive, pharmaceuticals and energy, and the model analyses the main choices implemented by these companies. Quantitative research techniques are used in combination with qualitative techniques to determine the drivers of resilience. We conducted many interviews in the companies in our sample, and we integrated that information with secondary data from business documents, institutional websites and newspaper articles.

We focused our interviews and data analysis on decision making in situations where top management teams are faced with such questions as: Is it better to be in a few markets in which we have a strong position or in many markets in which we may have less impact? Is it better to focus on a few products that make the company recognizable or diversify risk through the introduction of many products? Is it better to focus on the values of the founder or to try to be a global company in terms of culture and formulation? Is it better to prioritize the interests of shareholders or make products that appeal to the customer, even if the latter might reduce short-term performance? Is it better to decide quickly or listen to a number of opinions before arriving at a decision? Is it better to have specialist or generalist managers in the top management team?

Aligning on one side of the trade-off or the other can affect the company's ability to be resilient. Given the idiosyncratic decision-making challenges a company faces, the extant research has identified some drivers that increase the likelihood of obtaining positive, stable performance over time. These drivers, which should always be adapted to the specific environment in question,

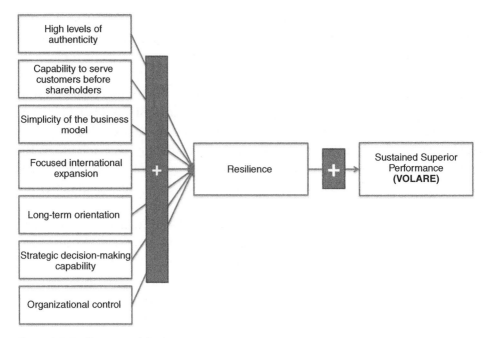

Figure 1.1 Resilience model
Source: authors' own

can be synthesized according to the model shown in Figure 1.1, which incorporates the assertions listed in the introduction:

1   Resilient companies show higher levels of authenticity. They approach the business in coherence with their traditions, competences, brand image and values.
2   Resilient companies have a high level of customer centricity. They are dedicated to the care of their customers and their needs, and they are willing to sacrifice short-term profitability in order to tie in customers in the long term. Employees identify with this strategy and are proud to be able to add value for customers before they think about shareholders.
3   Resilient companies have relatively simple business models and are determined to preserve key competencies by clearly linking their products and services to specific resources and capabilities.
4   Contrary to common beliefs, aggressive geographical diversification often increases the fragility of an organization, as it is difficult to assess and control all local risks. These problems increase with greater geographic diversification. Resilient companies hold a strong position in their

home markets and prefer to develop strong positions in a few additional markets as opposed to weak positions in many markets.

5   Decision makers in resilient companies employ a long-term perspective that goes beyond their mandate.

6   Leaders in resilient companies make strategic decisions. In addition, they manage to combine speed with quality of decisions.

7   Resilient companies are led by CEOs and relatively small top-management teams. Members of such teams have strong specialist and functional backgrounds, and they are bound by shared values.

Before we discuss each driver in detail, the next chapter focuses on how we can measure the performance implication of resiliency: SSP.

CHAPTER 2

Measuring Long-term Sustainable Performance

What are the main limitations of commonly used performance indicators? In other words, do we really need a new performance indicator to measure company success? Most performance indicators induce managers to focus on the short term and accept higher levels of risk. We therefore propose a new indicator, called VOLARE, which integrates existing performance indicators and allows us to uncover sustained superior performance (SSP). Companies that achieve SSP are the most resilient. VOLARE not only has an effect on stock prices, it changes the way in which business units can allocate resources and make *ex ante* assessments of the attractiveness of an industry or an investment.

THE LIMITATIONS OF COMMONLY USED PERFORMANCE INDICATORS

Probably one of the most effective ways of influencing the way that managers make decisions is to change the parameters with which performance indicators are selected and bonuses are calculated. Which performance measures should be used in business? The banking sector is able to calculate a variety of indicators and their impacts on strategy. All banks listed in Table 2.1, with the exceptions of UBS and Lloyds, can be said to be 'the best' according to at least one performance indicator. The Bank of America is first in terms of revenue, but if we consider EBIT (earnings before interest and taxes), the lead bank becomes CitiGroup. UBS, which appears second based on ROE (return on equity) in 2010, and Lloyds, which is third based on ROE from 2000 to 2010, are also close to the top according to at least one parameter. The question that Table 2.1 gives rise to is: Which performance category should be maximized?

The first step in raising the level of firm resilience is knowing how to measure it properly. There is no test for resilience if there are no external shocks. However, given the economic and financial crises that are disrupting the environment in which companies operate, this condition is unfortunately

Table 2.1 **The variety of performance indicators: the banking example**

Figures in USD	BBVA	Bank of Nova Scotia	Banco Santander	Hudson City Bancorp	Bank of America	Lloyds	UBS	Citigroup
Revenue 2010	5th (21,663 Mln)	7th (15,715 Mln)	3rd (67,387 Mln)	8th (2,947 Mln)	1st (134,194 Mln)	4th (41,750 Mln)	6th (18,873 Mln)	2nd (111,465 Mln)
EBIT 2010	4th (6,835 Mln)	5th (4,449 Mln)	2nd (12,052 Mln)	6th (892 Mln)	8th (-1,323 Mln)	7th (281 Mln)	3rd (8900.45 Mln)	1st (13,184 Mln)
EVA* 2010	3rd (-2,050 Mln)	1st (1,137 Mln)	5th (-5,336 Mln)	2nd (151.28 Mln)	8th (-27,345 Mln)	7th (-10,776 Mln)	4th (-3,901 Mln)	6th (-8,900 Mln)
TSR** (1 year) 2009–2010	3rd (59%)	2nd (81%)	1st (86%)	4th (25%)	6th (7.2%)	7th (-9%)	5th (11.4%)	8th (-50%)
Long Term TSR (10 years) 2000–2010	5th (36%)	2nd (524%)	3rd (230%)	1st (630%)	7th (14%)	8th (-49%)	6th (29%)	4th (208%)
RoE 2010	3rd (15.32%)	1st (20.2%)	4th (11.42%)	5th (9.90%)	8th (-1.77%)	7th (-0.72%)	2nd (16.7%)	6th (6.67%)
Average RoE 2000–2010	1st (29.99%)	2nd (24.78%)	4th (21.79%)	7th (10.53%)	5th (19.37%)	3rd (23.46%)	8th (8.78%)	6th (13%)

* EVA (economic value added = NOPAT – (WACC x equity).
** TSR (total shareholder return) = (2010 dividends + 2010 share price – 2009 share price)/2009 share price.

more persistent than ever. Above all, there can be no resilience without adopting a long-term perspective and without considering the risk associated with that perspective. As mentioned in Chapter 1, resilience is defined as the process by which firms make strategic decisions that increase their robustness, recovery and resourcefulness, and thereby ensure stable and consistent performance over time. This ability can only be evaluated when considering the medium- to long-term horizon. Like all performance indicators, we can only assess the performance of the past with the hope of gleaning information that will assist in upcoming business decisions. Notably, most performance indicators commonly used by companies actually only refer to the short term.

The measurement of performance using the correct variables serves as the methodological basis for building organizational resilience. *Moneyball*, Michael Lewis's bestseller (Lewis, 2004), describes how the Oakland Athletics (OA), an American baseball team, selected the appropriate indicators to enable the managers to inexpensively build a winning team. Prior to the adoption of the new method, OA based its decisions on the opinions of scouts, who viewed players as the first unit of measure. As such, they assessed their abilities to run, throw and hit. As a result, the team started losing games. The indicators used by the scouts no longer appeared to work. The team found itself in a state of crisis. It sold its top talent but could not afford to acquire great substitutes. Billy Beane, the team's general manager, proposed recruiting based on a different set of calculations developed with the help of the young economist Peter Brand. Brand argued that assessing the batting average of individual players was not important. Rather, it was more important to analyse their ability to get to first base. The players, coaches, fans, commentators and the whole world of baseball were sceptical and critical of this approach, especially in the beginning when losses continued. Eventually, however, OA beat every record for consecutive victories, as many as twenty, and the team was on the verge of the final victory of the season.

The book was published in the early 2000s, but its main message has not yet been fully embraced by companies. The majority of managers continue to rely on poorly selected statistics (Mauboussin, 2012). The problem may be related to the cognitive limitations of the people who have to use the performance indicators or the limitations of the indicators themselves. A person can make errors of judgment due to excessive confidence in their own analytical abilities (overconfidence bias), a low propensity to question the most common practices (status quo bias) or a tendency to use simple indicators that are already available (availability bias) (Mauboussin, 2012). However, in our study of resilience, we are more interested in the limitations of the indicators themselves.

Numerous factors highlighted in the literature (Pintea, 2012) should help managers design an appropriate set of performance indicators. Such indicators should be linked to the business strategy, and they should measure results rather than their causes. They should be timely. Moreover, they should be multidimensional, and they should detect the effects of interdependent actions. Indirect parameters lend themselves to manipulation and almost all of them are based on a short-term perspective. Many managers attempt to optimize economic measures, such as ROE, ROA (return on assets) or absolute EBIT. These measures provide an indication of economic performance in the previous year, but they are not able to take the medium- and long-term effects of past decisions into account. If we want sustainable performance, we must begin to measure it.

Some CEOs try to maximize revenue, given that company size seems to be correlated with the ability to pay higher wages and offer more opportunities to pander to the egos of top managers. Other companies maximize EBIT and cash flow, as this serves as a basis for paying dividends, making investments and repaying debt. The few companies that still try to maximize EVA (economic value added) seek returns greater than their cost of capital, sometimes through an increase in the debt/equity ratio and through strategies that boost short-term results. Top managers whose performance is measured on the basis of total shareholder return (TSR) try to nurture analysts' and investors' dreams of growth. As share prices are greatly influenced by the expectations of investors, companies have only minimal control over TSR in the short term. If they are good at creating high expectations and are, therefore, able to push stock prices higher than their real value, they risk shareholders becoming dissatisfied when they realize that their expectations were inflated. Table 2.2 summarizes the benefits and shortcomings of traditional performance measures.

All of the indicators described above can be viewed as VOLARE complements: they give short-term, limited information that is subject to fluctuations (i.e. due to new accounting policies or to shifts in the firm's industry). This makes it impossible to reach reliable conclusions about the performance of a company in a given period of time. As Table 2.2 shows, the *short-term perspective* is not the

Table 2.2 Benefits and shortcomings of performance measures

Performance Measures	Benefits	Concerns
ROE (return on equity)	★ One of the most important accounting figures, as it shows the return achieved with shareholder-entrusted resources. ★ To assess the strength of a ROE, one can apply the DuPont equation,[1] as it incorporates the impact of taxes, interest, return on sales, sales turnover and leverage on operations. If a DuPont equation ROE is low, managers can trace the element of the business that is underperforming – taxes, interest, return on sales, sales turnover or leverage.	★ Net income – a component of ROE – can fluctuate greatly due to the application of different accounting standards (e.g. IFRS, US GAAP, accrual adjustments).[2] ★ The use of different accounting principles and assumptions affects ROE's transparency and explanatory power. ★ As an accounting figure, the ratio has a short-term, historical focus. ★ The ratio does not address financial-risk considerations very well. ★ Growing debt leverage and stock buybacks can maintain a firm's ROE even if profitability is falling.

[1] The DuPont equation breaks ROE down into the following components:

$$ROE = \frac{Net\ Income}{Equity} = \frac{Net\ Income}{Pretax\ Income} \times \frac{Pretax\ Income}{EBIT} \times \frac{EBIT}{Sales} \times \frac{Sales}{Assets} \times \frac{Assets}{Equity}.$$

[2] Accrual accounting adjustments are defined as the transfer of 'costs and revenues between accounting periods' (Simons, 2000).

Table 2.2 (cont.)

Performance Measures	Benefits	Concerns
TSR (total shareholder return)	★ A simple method for monitoring developments in the firm's value by adding paid dividends to the change in share price over a certain period of time. ★ Like ROE and EVA, TSR is fully focused on value creation for the shareholder. ★ Unlike ROE or EVA, TSR considers the future performance of the company rather than the past. Based on shareholders' expectations, TSR forms an aggregated value analysis of a company.	★ A firm's value depends on the motives of investors. Thus, ownership structure and investment horizons can drive TSR, thereby limiting management's influence. ★ The embedding of TSR in the incentive system can misguide management, as shareholders might not be interested in the long-term success of the company. ★ Although long-term TSR might correct for volatility, majority owner groups may influence a firm's strategy. ★ TSR can only be calculated for publicly traded firms.
EBITDA (earnings before interest, taxes, depreciation and amortization)	★ Represents non-accrual operating earnings in the income statement. ★ Due to the exclusion of interest, taxes, depreciation and amortization (factors dependent on the firm's capital structure and accrual principles), EBITDA can be compared within industries. ★ EBITDA multiples are often used to determine the value of a company.	★ Even though EBITDA is useful for analysing the operations of a company, interest, taxes, depreciation and amortization need to be considered, as they can significantly influence the net income of a company as well as shareholder value creation.
EVA (economic value added)	★ This residual income concept is correlated with the stock price and shareholder value creation. A positive EVA signifies that capital is available for reinvestment or shareholder reimbursement above the level of expected return. ★ Can be incorporated into managers' bonus models to incentivize shareholder value creation. ★ With EVA adjustments, the accounting income is corrected for distortions arising from accrual accounting.	★ EVA adjustments are costly and time consuming, and adjustments are subjective (Arnold, 2008). ★ EVA is difficult to apply for knowledge-intensive firms with several business units. ★ As EVA is calculated on an annual basis, it tends to result in a short-term mind-set. ★ EVA does not consider competitors' and the industry's performance.

Table 2.2 (cont.)

Performance Measures	Benefits	Concerns
Balanced scorecard	★ Through the combination of outcome measures and performance drivers in the four perspectives[3] of the firm, the business strategy can be closely monitored and cause-and-effect relationships can be identified.	★ A complex and interlinked system of performance measures. It requires a profound understanding of the business mechanisms to reach the predefined long-term strategic objectives. ★ Constant monitoring and interpretation are time consuming and costly. ★ It does not replace other performance measures, as it focuses only on those factors, 'where high performance levels can be expected to lead to competitive breakthroughs' (Simons, 2000, p. 202).

only limitation of these performance indicators. Generally, these measures do not take a company's risk exposure into account. Even the average ten-year ROE is unable to provide feedback on actual performance that is linked to the volatility of results as a *measure of risk*. However, informed investors make decisions on where to invest based on the risk/return profile of an investment opportunity. For example, small investors who have to choose between buying Greek and German bonds at the same rate of interest will surely choose the less risky German bonds.

After the 2008 crisis, many companies divested risky activities or those not directly related to their core businesses. In 2012, Kodak announced that it would cease making digital cameras, pocket video cameras and digital picture frames, and instead focus on the corporate digital-imaging market (Rochester Business Journal, 2012).[4]

MEASURING SUSTAINED SUPERIOR PERFORMANCE: VOLATILITY AND ROE (VOLARE)

Based on these considerations, we propose a new measure of resilience called VOLARE, which complements existing indicators by including a long-term, risk-adjusted performance indicator. VOLARE (**Vol**atility **A**nd **R**OE) applies

---

[3] According to Simons (2000), there are four perspectives of a firm: the financial, the customer, the innovation and learning, and the internal business.
[4] See 'How Kodak lost its way' at: www.rbj.net/article.asp?aID=190212.

an investment approach that considers both the long-term ROE (as a measure of profitability), which we define as the average ROE over a ten-year period, and the volatility of ROE (as a measure of risk).

Specifically:

$$ROE_{LT} = \frac{Net\ Income_{Av.10y}}{Equity_{Av.10y}}.$$

$$Volatility_{ROE} = \sqrt{\frac{1}{n}\sum_{i=1}^{n}(x_i - \bar{x})'}.$$

Where n is the size of the sample and $\bar{x}$ is the arithmetic mean of the sample. Our decision to use ROE as an indicator is based on the fact that it is less dependent on market expectations or perceptions. For example, stock prices are influenced by investor expectations, while TSR is not directly controllable by companies because it is based on the perceptions of analysts and investors. However, the VOLARE logic can be replicated using other performance indicators, such as free cash flow or ROA, as a basis.

Inspired by the model developed by Markowitz (1959), and taking into account both the ROE over a ten-year period and the volatility of ROE for the same period, VOLARE serves as a proxy of resilience or, more precisely, of superior sustained performance (SSP) over time. To identify the level of resilience of each company in a given sector, the long-term ROE and volatility are represented on a graph (Figure 2.1). The highest values of the long-term ROE for a selected interval of volatility are identified and linked through logarithmic regression. The resulting curve is called VOLARE 10. The companies on this curve are the most resilient. The companies most distant from this curve are those with lower resilience (VOLARE 0).

ISO curves are created to measure the levels of VOLARE and are plotted by lowering the curve by 4 per cent. The areas of VOLARE are delineated, allowing the long-term ROE to vary by +/-2 per cent for the same standard deviation. The construction of the VOLARE measure allows us to code the 705 companies in our database according to their level of VOLARE (from 0 to 10) in the period 2002 to 2011. The data were derived from Reuters. We considered the following industries: automotive, food and beverages, banking, pharmaceuticals, telecommunications, energy and household appliances.

VOLARE allows us to assign a score from 0 to 10 (where 0 is the lowest and 10 the highest) to companies in the different industries. In the automotive industry, for example, leaders in our sample include Audi, Porsche and Hyundai (Figure 2.1). In the pharmaceutical sector, Novo Nordisk leads the

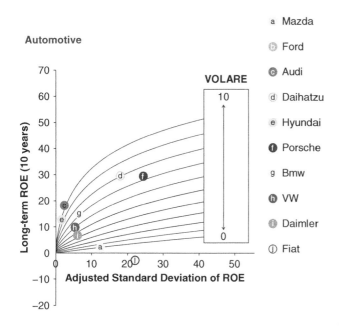

Figure 2.1 VOLARE in the automotive industry
Source: authors' own based on Reuters data

pack. Among the banks, the Bank of Nova Scotia and Banco Santander are at the top of the list. The database enables us to map the resilient companies in the period 2001–2010 and to compare them with those that were unable to react well to the external shocks.

VOLARE AND THE EFFECT ON THE STOCK EXCHANGE

Prior to defining what makes a company more or less resilient, we investigate whether more resilient companies have more stable share prices than more vulnerable companies. To measure the effect of an external shock on share prices, we identified the minimum price after a shock for a sample of 304 top firms active in the banking, apparel, publishing and automotive sectors, and compared that minimum price to the share price one year before and one year after that moment. The results were surprising – the share prices of companies with the highest VOLARE fell by approximately the same percentages as those of companies with low VOLARE. There are three ways to interpret this phenomenon: VOLARE is not a good measure of resilience, it takes a long time for companies to activate their potential for resilience or the financial

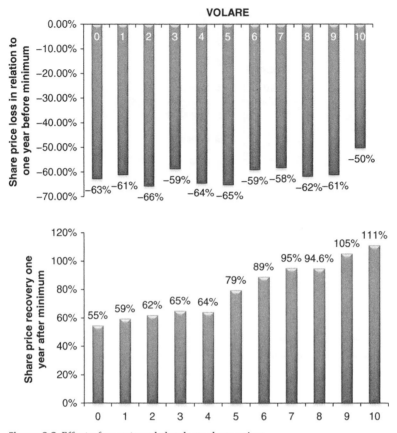

Figure 2.2 Effect of an external shock on share prices
Source: authors' own

market does not consider individual companies when share prices drop across an industry (Figure 2.2).

However, an indication of the robustness of VOLARE as a measure of resilience is evident in the lower part of Figure 2.2. As the graph shows, the share prices of companies with high VOLARE recover more quickly than those with low VOLARE.

Initially, the market does not seem to be particularly well informed with respect to what is happening. In the face of a crisis, the market indiscriminately punishes all firms in an industry. The only indication in this case seems to be to 'sell, sell, sell'. Over time, however, the market becomes aware of the top companies, and many investors 'fly to quality'. The ability to recover with respect to share price is also an element of resilience, as ROE and share price need to be correlated in the long run.

HOW VOLARE CHANGES RESOURCE ALLOCATION

The crisis has shown that companies should create more robust business models. However, the goal of developing resilience seems to be a strategic priority only after a shock has occurred. Many companies seem to have already forgotten the effects of the 2008 crisis, and many have returned to their old ways of doing business with positive results. However, up to what point can we consider ourselves safe? The 'new normal' has been coined as the latest buzzword. It suggests that the equilibrium is only fictitious, and that another bubble can burst or a shock can manifest at any moment. The crisis is not over – we have simply learned to live with it. However, few companies are truly fit to face the bursting of a new bubble. After the Asian tsunami disaster in 2004, numerous earthquakes subsequently hit the Thai coast, bringing successive waves. While the first wave created tremendous damage, the latter waves worsened the situation.

VOLARE forces companies to undertake some *ex ante* assessments, namely before a shock occurs, and guides them towards less fallacious judgments. Is it more advantageous to invest in an investment bank that provides a higher return or in a retail bank that provides a lower yield? The investment bank might seem more attractive in the short term, but it could be riskier in the long term. VOLARE, which allows for consideration of both profitability and risk, shows that the retail bank is a more secure investment, albeit one with a lower yield. In this way, VOLARE, with its risk/return consideration, orients the allocation of resources not only at the level of individual projects but also at the level of entire business units towards investments that are positive and stable over time.

Most managers probably assess risk in some way when they allocate their free cash flow to various businesses. We doubt that they only focus on higher profit or yields. Nevertheless, a more formal approach is needed that shows how the long-term risk/return performance of businesses supports more prudent managers who appreciate a balanced business portfolio. The calculation and communication of VOLARE to demanding shareholders at least makes risk/return trade-offs more transparent.

FROM VOLARE TO THE DRIVERS OF RESILIENCE

Given the relative scarcity of literature on the process that leads to resilience in companies, we opted to use inductive theory based on the selection of multiple case studies (Eisenhardt and Graebner, 2007) to identify the drivers of resilience. The cases were taken from the VOLARE database using a non-random sampling technique. Random sampling is appropriate for deductive research and subsequent statistical analysis. In inductive research, each case is chosen to assist in the construction of a theoretical model, moving from the identification of a phenomenon to its insertion in precise conceptual categories.

To avoid the halo effect (Rosenzweig, 2007) and not only consider cases of success, we selected companies with high (values of 10 or 9) and low (0 or 1) VOLARE. For each sector, we considered at least two companies with high VOLARE and two with low VOLARE, which gives a total 32 companies. We used several data sources:

★ interviews,
★ email and telephone follow-up calls, and
★ secondary data gathered from such sources as the media, the Internet and corporate materials.

The semi-structured interviews were carried out with different informants: CEOs, CFOs and first-line managers. Each interview lasted 45–90 minutes, and was recorded and later transcribed. Every interview focused on the shocks that had affected the sectors in which the focal company operated, a comparison of the company's VOLARE with those of competitors and the formation of the main drivers of resilience. To avoid common-response anchoring, we employed several widely utilized techniques. First, we used different sources and informants. Second, questions were open-ended and did not, in any way, suggest possible answers. Third, the questions were based on facts and hard data regarding what respondents had done or seen collaborators/competitors do. Given our reliance on the inductive method (Eisenhardt and Graebner, 2007), we carried out the interviews and integrated the data they provided with follow-up data without making *a priori* assumptions. Therefore, the definitions and conclusions we reached were derived from the information obtained during the data-collection process. After the main drivers had been identified, we compared the emerging theoretical framework with extant literature on the research theme to refine the variable and the theoretical relations of the construct. Specific attention was paid to certain practices that are particularly illustrative in terms of strategic and managerial models.

The following chapters describe the different drivers in our model. In other words, they cover the organizational and strategic variables that can determine a company's resilience.

CHAPTER 3

Authenticity

Famous films, such as *Braveheart*, have spread the idea that ancient Scots wore kilts and that bagpipes sounded across ancient Scotland. In reality, the history of the kilt is much more recent – the garment did not even exist in the Middle Ages. It was invented much later, in the early 1700s. Moreover, the instrument most widely played in the Wallace years was probably the Irish harp.

In 1727, the British began to exploit the forests of the Scottish Highland settlements for stocks of timber, and the Scots were hired to work in the kilns that produced coal. The garment commonly worn by the Scots at that point was not particularly suitable for working with machinery. It was then that an Anglo-Saxon magnate by the name of Rawlingstone designed the more practical kilt.

In 1747, the Disarming Act banned the kilt, and for the next fifty years it was not worn. In fact, most forgot about it. At the end of the century, nobles and intellectuals repealed the law, and had refined versions woven. The memory of the kilt was, in fact, kept alive by the Scottish military, which the British engaged for the wars in the colonies. The soldiers of the Highlands were necessarily immune to the Disarming Act. In order to distinguish themselves from other armies, the soldiers in these units wore kilts. As a result, Scottish nobles – and the imagery of the era – began to view this garment as the symbol of a nation that would not give up.

Sir Walter Scott was head of the Celtic Society of Edinburgh, a group of nostalgics who evoked the nation's past by wearing kilts. In 1822, King George IV of England planned an official visit to Edinburgh. A group of conspirators sewed thousands of kilts, allocating a pattern to each visiting clan. Upon his arrival, George IV was convinced that kilts were a centuries-old tradition – a tradition that spanned thousands of years, perhaps – and from that day forth, he and all of England were enchanted by a romantic invention sustained by economic interest.

The job of cementing the kilt's place in Scottish heritage fell to the Allen brothers, two mid-nineteenth-century noblemen. In 1842, they rediscovered *Vestiarium Scoticum*, an ancient text from dubious sources that quoted real and fictional texts, and included illustrations of each clan's tartan. Although revised, the Allen brothers' Vestiarium served as the real pattern for the modern kilt.[1]

The history of the Scottish kilt illustrates the importance of symbols that represent us in an authentic way. Even though the kilt does not have a long tradition, we like to believe that an authentic Scotsman wears (or at least owns) a kilt. Although the concept of authenticity in history has been discussed by leading philosophers (Heidegger, 1927; Sartre, 1943), it has only recently been applied for the purpose of explaining business success.

Kierkegaard, in the first half of the nineteenth century, suggested that those who believe in something that is wrong but do so sincerely and genuinely would be saved, while those who inauthentically and with little conviction believe in something that is right would not. Heidegger adopted the two concepts and applied them to existence. In analysing the meaning of the words, he pointed out that the word 'authentic' encompasses the Greek root *autos*, which means 'self'. A thing, therefore, is authentic when it is itself – when it is its own to the end. One can talk about authentic existence when the being (the object of existence) makes true choices or, more precisely, 'authentic' choices. In other words, authenticity arises when the being puts itself at stake through its choices. Conversely, an existence is inauthentic when it is characterized by non-choices.

Not surprisingly, modern times have brought a renewed interest in authenticity. Existentialism, the philosophical-literary movement that had its greatest exponent in Sartre, criticized romantic optimism (based on the recognition of some absolute values) and proposed the philosophy of anxiety, or the crisis. This view represents man as a finite being thrown into the world and abandoned to the determinism of his choices. The central theme among existentialists is that existence is a way of being that is described as a relationship with the self, others, the world, things and God. This existential relationship requires man to make choices or undertake projects susceptible to risk. Existentialists believe that man is not a substantial, pre-determined reality, but rather an entity who faces certain possibilities of realization that engage his freedom, and are at the two extremes of authenticity and inauthenticity.

---

[1] https://en.wikipedia.org/wiki/Vestiarium_Scoticum.

Making choices means living an authentic life in which man is brought into play as an individual and called upon as such. Therefore, no one man can make decisions for another.

The current situation seems very similar to the existentialist perspective. We are once again facing a crisis, and we have to make choices in order to overcome it and survive it. The sociologist Gary Alan Fine wrote: 'The desire for authenticity now occupies a central position in contemporary culture. Whether in our search for selfhood, leisure experiences, or in our material purchases, we search for the real, the genuine, (Fine, 2001, p. 153).

We see it in commercials, shop signs and business meetings – the word 'authentic' is used a great deal, especially in these years of crisis. There seems to be a kind of modern obsession with defining what is authentic. This is evident in mass-media news, which gives glimpses of the private lives of politicians. The public wants to know what really happens behind the scenes, what lies behind the official. We see it in marketing, with Coca-Cola's slogan 'The Real Thing' followed by Starbucks calling its lunch salads 'Real Food'. Marks and Spencer, a well-known UK brand specializing in clothing, cosmetics and gifts, claims to sell 'authentic clothing' and 'authentic apparel', especially in reference to a line of leisure clothing for men inspired by Cornwall on the southern coast of England. This line of clothing for men includes boxer shorts, which automatically become 'authentic boxers'.

Authenticity adapts particularly well to the food and beverage sector. Cities are filled with signboards advertising 'authentic' breweries that produce craft beers in contrast to those produced on an industrial scale, or for Trappist beers produced by monks in the monasteries of Belgium and the Netherlands. Authentic food, following the same logic, is organic and without preservatives.

In fashion, the issue is even more heartfelt. Consider, for example, a 'real' Gucci bag as opposed to a black-market imitation. Customers are willing to pay a higher price to ensure the authenticity of the brand. Authenticity is also referred to in fiction. Many award-winning films claim to be based on true stories. This is the case of the 2012 film *Zero Dark Thirty* directed by Kathryn Bigelow and nominated for five Oscars, which tells of the raid that led to the killing of Osama Bin Laden. Even literary classics utilize this tactic. *Robinson Crusoe* (1719), for example, begins with the statement 'written by himself' to convey the impression of a personal diary.

In politics or in reality shows, contenders try to beat opponents accusing them of 'not much truth'. They all claim to be on the side of what is right and what is real. In politicians' speeches, we often hear statements along the lines of 'my party is realistic, while the opponent's party is based on unrealistic utopian visions'. In the famous Big Brother reality show, the confessional was invented. It took the form of a room in which competitors could isolate themselves from others and talk to the public 'in private', precisely to create a genuine arena for truthful conversation.

There is also a growing market for authentic, hyper-realistic films and television shows showing real life and scenes filmed 'in the first person'. For some, this has come as a surprise. The television presenter and actress Oprah Winfrey stated: 'I had no idea that being your authentic self could make me as rich as I've become. If I had, I'd have done it a lot earlier.'

DISCOVERING AUTHENTICITY

According to Glenn Carroll, a professor at Stanford University, there are two categories of authenticity. The first is 'type authenticity': the more one is identifiable with a class or a specific type (e.g. product, market, customer segment), the more authentic one is. In this case, a firm is authentic if it is focused on a specific product, market segment or area. The second is 'moral authenticity': the more one is identifiable with some predetermined reference values, the more authentic one is. Lance Secretan[2] states that 'authenticity is the alignment of head, mouth, heart, and feet – thinking, saying, feeling, and doing the same thing – consistently. This builds trust, and followers love leaders they can trust'.

A business is authentic if it reflects values and specific traditions. Values can be established by the founder, given by the country of origin or acquired over time. The important thing is that the type in the first case and value assets in the second must be clearly definable and recognizable.

Authenticity is not a concept that exists in itself. Instead, it is always given by the perceptions of an audience, a public or another group of actors who judge and cognitively recognize the characteristics of authenticity of a subject, such as a firm. Authenticity always involves a relationship between two parties and, consequently, one subject's evaluation of another. In other words, for a business to be defined as genuine, a set of actors must express a judgment of that business. The firm is evaluated by a series of social partners – customers,

---

[2] Lance H.K. Secretan is known for his work on leadership theory and inspiring teams. Formerly managing director of Manpower Limited, he taught leadership at McMaster and York universities in Canada. Since 1985, he has worked as an author, independent management consultant, coach and keynote speaker.

employees and the media – and these partners decide its authenticity. The judgments of these stakeholders are increasingly taken into account, as the firm's long-term performance depends on them. Our observations suggest that the more a company is evaluated as authentic in terms of type and moral values, the more resilient it will be over time. Let us analyse the two categories in relation to organizational resilience.

TYPE AUTHENTICITY

Type authenticity explains why a product and/or market focus increases the resilience of businesses from a sociological perspective. Companies focused on a few products in clearly defined segments (see Chapter 6) or on coherent market sectors (see Chapter 7) seem to perfectly adhere to the classification assigned to them by consumers and to consumers' expectations. They thereby manage to ensure sustained superior performance (SSP) over time. More specifically, type authenticity allows the firm to focus on a few core competencies in coherence with the business. In a firm active in the energy sector, for example, core competencies are of the technological and engineering type. In turn, core competencies make the company and its top management recognizable, and send a unique, reassuring message. It is easier to trust something that can be precisely defined.

This is a little like dining at a Chinese restaurant, where you would expect to find spring rolls on the menu and red lanterns hanging from the walls. If you recognize these elements at the entrance of the restaurant, you will enter more willingly because you already know what to expect. Fusion or creative restaurants that combine different types of cuisine can prove to be the best dining experience in the world, but they initially generate hesitation and uncertainty among potential customers. Each type of restaurant – and each company – must have some recognizable features. The inclusion of pizza in a sushi bar will create some perplexities. In order to communicate values of belonging, companies use trademarks or logos. Not surprisingly, the etymology of the word 'mark' derives from the Latin *marculus* (hammer). *Marculare*, or hammering, means leaving a mark. Thus, a trademark is a sign made to recognize or authenticate something.

The state of confusion caused by exposure to two different categories that cannot be distinguished from each other was studied by the Russian scientist Ivan Pavlov, who is primarily famous for his discovery of the conditioned reflex. In a cruel experiment undertaken in 1914, called the circle-ellipse, a dog was placed in front of an image with two buttons. If the image was a circle, the dog had to press button A. If it was an ellipse, button B had to be pressed. If the wrong button was pressed or no button was pressed within a specified period of time, an electric shock followed. Through the conditioned reflex, the dog learned to associate the image with the corresponding button and with the consequent absence of pain.

After the animal had learned the answers, an element of confusion was introduced by making the ellipse appear more like a circle on each successive presentation until the dog could no longer distinguish it from a circle. The dog then entered into the sought-after state of confusion and tried to figure out how to respond. In the face of this systematic uncertainty, one of three types of action strategies unfailingly manifested:

★ The dog refused to respond and suffered the shocks given his indifference to avoiding them.
★ The dog tried to respond correctly, attempting to refine or elaborate associations that allowed him to avoid the shocks.
★ The dog responded randomly and seemed indifferent to the associations that the visual stimulus evoked.

The induced confusion between the two categories – the circle and ellipse – created exactly the same effects as schizophrenia according to the Kraepelin study. One might say that companies also risk schizophrenia if they focus on a variety of businesses that are not clearly defined.

The case of Starbucks is interesting. Starbucks, one of the world's most famous coffee companies, was founded in Seattle more than thirty years ago. It has thousands of outlets around the world. In each geographical market, from New York to Tokyo, the company's basic idea is always the same: export the model of authenticity of Italian coffee bars and promote a unique experience for the consumer, that of the 'third place'. Starbucks established itself over time as the third meeting place beyond home and work, and as a relaxing and familiar place where customers could feel good.

However, in 2008, the coffee chain experienced a crisis. It closed more than 600 outlets in the United States with the loss of 12,000 jobs. The CEO, Howard Schultz, stated that the company had not only lost in terms of results, but also, in a sense, in terms of identity. It no longer knew how to define itself or in which direction to move. In its effort to rediscover type authenticity, the idea for the 'mystarbucksidea.com' platform was born. This platform asked customers to indicate which products or services could be implemented to allow Starbucks to regain its authenticity. The success of the initiative was huge and was multiplied on a global scale, returning Starbucks to good performance. In addition, for twenty years, Howard Schultz tried to find a good way to sell the Yankee version of enjoying coffee in Italy, where coffee is rooted in very strong traditions. In 2015, he announced that Starbucks had found an original formula based on the use of digital media to capture the attention of Italian customers. The idea is to select locations in city centres that attract bankers, lawyers, entrepreneurs and professionals who would like to talk in confidence and have good Wi-Fi access. Moreover, the company developed the *Starbucks Digital Network*, which offers such content as films, television series and news for a relaxing and entertaining break dedicated to the company's youngest customers.[3]

When faced with flattening beer sales in its extended home markets in Europe, the Danish beer brewer Carlsberg had to search for new growth avenues without losing its type authenticity. Like many brewers, Carlsberg had increasingly branched out to offer more varieties of non- or low-alcoholic beers, ciders, and malt-based, non-alcoholic beverages. Similarly, Heineken introduced at least ten non-alcoholic beer brands and varieties in its home market of the Netherlands, in Italy and elsewhere between 2008 and 2011. AB InBev started to tap a non-alcoholic version of its Hoegaarden brand in its home turf of Belgium. It also launched 'Jupiler Force' – a non-alcoholic, brewed soft drink that tasted like pilsner.[4] Brewers were also trying to capitalize on the health trend and to attract more women.

Carlsberg's core business has always been beer, and the company's core competences were focused on cereals/grain, yeast, fermentation and brewing. Thus, Carlsberg's strategy required that innovations and new products build on these core competences, and focus primarily on beer and adjacent new platforms.[5] One such platform was the cider category. In 2007, Carlsberg successfully launched a new cider called 'Somersby'; in the Nordic markets. Somersby Cider, which came in two varieties (apple and pear), was positioned as an alternative to beer or white wine. Benefitting from the recent rebirth of the category (e.g. *The Guardian* newspaper proclaimed cider 'the new Chardonnay'), sales rose quickly.[6] The product line was later extended with the addition of new flavours.[7] Carlsberg also started looking at the non-alcoholic beer segment, as Lene Dyrby Andersen, an executive handling new-product development, noted: 'Non-alcoholic beer is a largely

---

[3] See 'Starbucks in Italia' at: http://fortune.com/2016/02/28/starbucks-italy/.

[4] *The Wall Street Journal Europe*, 'As Europe's beer sales go flat, brewers remove the alcohol,' 30 August 2011, www.pressreader.com/belgium/the-wall-street-journal-europe/20110830/281994669195517.

[5] Carlsberg Annual Report, 2010.

[6] Ibid.

[7] Somersby Cider website, www.somersbycider.com.

unexploited opportunity for big brewers. It is quite a natural move when you see that the overall beer markets [in Western Europe] are going down. So of course we're battling for market share.'[8] In addition to rolling out new varieties of non-alcoholic beer in Norway, Finland and other countries, Carlsberg reformulated its German 'Holsten Alkoholfrei' to taste more like a traditional brew. Moreover, it introduced two flavours (orange-hibiscus and apple-green tea) of its 'Beo' non-alcoholic soft drink, which was brewed like a beer and mixed with fruit juice.[9]

Carlsberg was equally interested in the industry's quest for female consumers, as 80 per cent of Carlsberg's 2010 global volume was consumed by men, while women made up half of the world's population and accounted for more than one-third of all alcohol consumption.[10] Carlsberg tried to make up for its previous lack of focus on women by introducing new drinks that targeted women – either directly or on a unisex platform. These drinks included Somersby, Baltika Cooler and Kronenbourg 1664.[11] Designed exclusively for women and packaged in an elegant 'feminine' bottle, 'Eve' was targeted at females aged 25–35. Although brewed on a beer base, it had a fruit flavour (lychee, passion fruit or grapefruit) and a relatively low percentage of alcohol (3.1%). Originally innovated by Carlsberg's Swiss subsidiary in 2006, Eve was launched in various markets across the geographical portfolio by 2010, including the United Kingdom, Denmark, Russia and Vietnam.[12]

In 2011, Carlsberg launched 'Copenhagen', a Danish beer with international appeal, as the 'first innovative offering for the new generation of beer drinkers who delight in the full package of design, taste and quality'.[13] Copenhagen was targeted at modern women and men who appreciated a refreshing taste delivered in a stylish design. The move reflected Carlsberg's strategy to sharpen its focus on the innovation and development of new products that could be sold across the world. Copenhagen was the first new beer, brand and design developed by Carlsberg's centralized International

---

[8] *The Wall Street Journal Europe*, 'As Europe's beer sales go flat, brewers remove the alcohol,' 30 August 2011, www.pressreader.com/belgium/the-wall-street-journal-europe/20110830/ 281994669195517.

[9] Ibid.

[10] See www.cnbc.com/id/43107702.

[11] Ibid.

[12] Carlsberg Annual Report, 2010.

[13] Carlsberg Group website, Media, Press Room, Copenhagen, www.carlsberggroup.com/media/ IntheMedia/Pages/Copenhagen%E2%80%93ADanishbeerwithInternationalappeal.aspx.

Innovation Department in collaboration with the Carlsberg Research Centre, and it was to be rolled out globally.[14]

In addition to new product development and innovation, Carlsberg's Global Marketing, Sales and Innovation department invested heavily in a major repositioning of its flagship premium brand, Carlsberg, which was supported by a range of new marketing initiatives. In April 2011, the relaunch was rolled out simultaneously across more than 140 markets.[15] The aim of the effort was to unleash the brand's full potential with the goal of doubling the brand's profits by 2015.[16] Carlsberg abandoned its slogan of 'Probably the best beer in the world' and replaced it with a new global tag line, 'That calls for a Carlsberg'. The company was attempting to emphasize its heritage and values while connecting with an active, adventurous generation of consumers, encouraging them 'to step up and do the right thing' with a Carlsberg beer as a reward. One objective was to anchor a single selling line and visual identity for the Carlsberg brand in all markets.[17] Another objective was to capture more market share in the lucrative premium end of the beer market, especially as profit margins were increasingly under pressure in the industry.

In 2015, Carlsberg stretched its type authenticity by launching a line of male grooming products called 'Beer Beauty'. On its website, Carlsberg argues that 'we only use the finest yeasts, hops and barley in our world famous lager beer. And one day we realised that those ingredients are actually packed with Vitamin-B and Silicium, which is good for your hair and skin. So we decided to make our proprietary beer recipe, our proprietary beauty recipe. It's beauty from beer'.[18] The company appears to be attempting to establish a relationship between beer and cosmetics, as each product in the Beer Beauty series contains 0.5 litres of real Carlsberg beer. Only time will tell whether men will find beer-based grooming products attractive, and whether they will want to get their drinks from the same company as their shampoo.

Marco Pasetti is CEO of the historic Farmaceutici Dottor Ciccarelli pharmaceutical company, which is perfectly in line with type authenticity. Its

---

[14] Ibid.

[15] Carlsberg Press Release, 'International makeover for iconic Carlsberg brand,' 5 April 2011, www.carlsberggroup.com/media/PressKits/Documents/Carlsberg/International_makeover_for _iconic_carlsberg_brand.pdf.

[16] Carlsberg Group website, Media, Press Kit, Carlsberg: That calls for a Carlsberg, www .carlsberggroup.com/media/PressKits/brands/carlsberg/Pages/Default.aspx.

[17] Carlsberg Press Release, 'International makeover for iconic Carlsberg brand,' 5 April 2011, www.carlsberggroup.com/media/PressKits/Documents/Carlsberg/International_makeover_for _iconic_carlsberg_brand.pdf.

[18] www.carlsberg.com/#!beer-beauty|beer-beauty/1476-yeast-hops-barley-beauty.

products, especially Pasta del Capitano toothpaste, have had a profound effect on the Italian socio-cultural evolution. In addition to the well-known oral hygiene brand, the company has created and maintained other solid brands, such as Cera di Cupra in women's cosmetics. Pasetti has a very clear vision of what needs to be done in order to be resilient:

> The myth of globalization has meant that many companies have lost their identities. To resist, especially in times of crisis, consistency is essential. When all our competitors lowered prices in Q1 2013, we did not, and the results proved us right. Sure, it was not easy, but it was worth it. You cannot always and only look for immediate profit. You must think and ponder the choices. Nerves of steel, in sum. And innovation. We have launched a new line of SOS-branded products for pharmacies, which are producing excellent results.[19]

MORAL AUTHENTICITY

Starbucks was able to identify a specific set of values or traditions, or in other words, what is called the organizational culture. 'Organizational culture' refers to all of the norms, values and beliefs that are an integral part of an organization. Typically, organizational culture is born from the ideas or beliefs of the person who founded the organization, which are transmitted internally over the years.

Culture is the set of basic assumptions, values, ideologies, opinions, knowledge and ways of thinking that are shared by the members of an organization. The observable elements of culture are:

1 The 'communication system', which can also be symbolic (e.g. how to talk, greet, establish relationships with others and dress).
2 Rites, ceremonies and planned collective activities characterized by high emotional involvement that take place in the presence of an audience (e.g. the introduction of new employees, salesperson of the month awards, introductions of new directors, management–employee meetings, Christmas dinners, corporate travel).
3 The physical elements of the organization, which can be particularly effective because they focus attention on a specific object (e.g. the shape of the building, the layout of the premises, uniforms).

[19] Il Mondo, 7 December 2013.

Corporate culture is transmitted through language, and is automatically reflected in the ways that people perceive, think and identify. Slogans and maxims can serve as a means of persuasively communicating a variety of meanings to organizational members. They might, for instance, be used to justify and explain events that happened in the past or existing situations. Organizational stories, especially employee anecdotes, stories for commercials and business documents, are very important.

In other words, culture allows the beliefs and core values of the organization to spread. Ethical values relate to the sphere of moral opinions that indicate what is right and what is wrong. Beliefs indicate the system of interpretations adopted by members of the organization with respect to internal and external events.

Researchers have often studied organizational culture as a relevant variable in analyses of firm performance. Typically, a well-defined organizational culture and shared values generate positive effects on performance. Kotter and Heskett (1992) argue that in an organization with a strong culture, members can work together to find common solutions and solve problems. Especially in very stressful contexts, sharing values makes it easier to withstand stress and obtain better results (Robbins, 1998). In several theoretical frameworks, ways of bringing culture across national borders are discussed. The emphasis placed on the emergence of multinational corporations has been supported by the conviction that an open, global culture can be the key factor in international success.

Along these lines, our research suggests that the imprinting of values has a significant impact on determining the resilience of organizations. Companies that are able to clearly define their value assets are more resilient.

In Ridley Scott's *Gladiator*, General Maximus Decimus Meridio, who is enslaved and fighting in the ranks of the gladiatorial arena to avenge the murder of his family and his emperor, urges the other gladiators to stay united. He speaks to the gladiators about the plan:

MAXIMUS: Anyone here been in the army?
FIRST FELLOW COMBATANT: Yes.
SECOND FELLOW COMBATANT: I served with you in Vindobona.
MAXIMUS: You can help me. Whatever comes out of those gates, we'll have a better chance of survival if we work together. Do you understand? We stay together, we survive.

(Excerpt of a dialogue from the film *Gladiator*)

Similarly, shared values and established routines enable an organization to be resilient. German automotive companies, for example, are recognized around the world for their values of innovation, efficiency and accuracy. In the 2016 Best Brand awards in Germany, Porsche is the winner for the 'Best Brands International' category, followed by BMW in second place.[20] At the same event, Nivea won the award for best product, mainly due to its 'back to its roots' strategy of returning to the original design of the first Nivea jar. Heinz, a giant in the food industry, is keen to be perceived in all of its communications as a company from Pittsburgh because the quality of life in Pittsburgh is high, just like the quality of Heinz products. Nestlé bases its success on the concepts of integrity, honesty and precision, which are essentially perceived as Swiss heritage par excellence. As the company's CEO, Paul Bulcke, states: 'The values of Nestlé are the basis of our corporate culture, developed over 140 years, which reflects the idea of fairness, honesty and long-term vision. These values are derived from our Swiss origins.'[21] We visited Nestlé's subsidiary in Moscow and were greeted by a Swiss manager who told us: 'Nestlé feels Swiss anywhere in the world, and consumers know that they can trust the brand.'

The imprinting of national values, which are exported as a trademark across the world, reflects the importance of authenticity. An organization is defined as authentic if it embodies the values determined by its founders, owners or members, and does not simply rely on conventions (Carroll and Wheaton, 2009). In this sense, the specialized Italian master-craft enterprises, recently surveyed in the context of a Bocconi University research project,[22] serve as good examples. These companies, most of which are small, intrinsically possess authenticity, originality, highly specialized know-how, and connections with traditions and specific territories, all of which are critical success factors. Despite the rising failure rate among other companies operating in the same arena caused by the crisis, these companies maintained or increased their level of investments (in 50.5% of cases) in the years of the crisis and maintained or raised their level of operating investments between 2012 and 2013 in the vast majority of the cases (66%). In addition, these companies maintained (55%) or raised (15%) the number of staff employed.

Similarly, when Italian, Spanish and Portuguese winemakers expanded and the French could no longer cope with the lower prices, Bordeaux winemakers

---

[20] See 'Best Brands 2016' at: www.serviceplan.com/en/news-detailed/bb2016-en.html.

[21] Nestlé's principles are available at: www.nestle.com/aboutus/businessprinciples.

[22] Dallocchio, M. and Vizzaccaro, M., *Valorizzazione del territorio e sviluppo delle eccellenze locali – Il saper fare italiano per il rilancio dell'economia*, forthcoming book.

began to focus on the authenticity of their products. This allowed them to charge a premium price. They unified the small *grands crus* into a few larger holdings and associated them with neighbouring country houses or chateaux, such as Pétrus, Margaux, Latour and Mouton-Rothschild. This marketing technique of positioning luxury wines as a product in direct contrast to mass-produced wines is still employed. French winemakers stress the historic style specific to the particular castle, or *terroir*, and thereby create a brand aura.

Similarly, in Italy there is a cross-sector segment of companies that can be defined as 'high-end'. Most of these companies possess both 'type authenticity' and 'moral authenticity' in some way. They have performed well mainly due to their strong connections with national values and traditions, a high propensity to innovate, and their dedication to quality (which are all elements typical of 'moral authenticity'). They are also characterized by a strategic, coherent and well-defined market focus (which is key for 'type authenticity'). When it comes to 'high-end', we refer (a) to the production of goods and services that are useful for everyday life, (b) to a specific company philosophy geared towards meeting the needs of a demanding consumer segment and (c) to the continuous improvement of products and production processes. Most high-end companies use selective distribution to operate globally, and they are generally innovative and offer high value-added. In addition, they tend to be characterized by high levels of creativity, design, and in-house production and craftsmanship. This business model has the potential to generate excellent results despite an economic downturn, as demonstrated by the results of a recent Bocconi University research project:

★ The employment generated by high-end companies in Italy totals 491,000 including both direct and indirect employment (2.14% of total employment in Italy as of 2012). These companies have 234 employees per firm on average, which can be compared to fifteen in other firms active in their sectors. The 'high end' is responsible for the indirect employment of 4.49 people for each employee directly employed, while the corresponding figure for the remaining part of the sectors is 0.97.

★ In terms of exports, high-end companies have proved to be more active on the international scene. On average, the high-end companies generate 49 per cent of their sales abroad, which can be compared to 27.4 per cent among the companies belonging to the remaining parts of these sectors.

★ From a fiscal point of view, the greater added value generated by high-end companies appears to result in more taxes on generated revenues (2.85%) than in the remaining part of the sectors (1.42%). The average value of taxes paid in 2012 amounted to about EUR 1.8 million per high-end firm. This figure stood at just EUR 40,000 for companies belonging to the remaining part of the sectors. This demonstrates the higher contribution to the development of national economy made by high-end companies.

★ High-end companies have also shown a higher level of investments, with an investment/turnover ratio of 7.67 per cent compared to 4.45 per cent for the remaining parts of the sectors. In terms of investment per employee, the high-end companies averaged EUR 24.54 per employee, which can be compared to EUR 17.03 for the remaining parts of the sectors.

High-end companies are characterized by a set of values and behaviours that create a specific corporate culture through a process of stratification over time. Well aware of the power of culture, many firms have invested massive amounts of energy in identifying a set of values and behavioural standards that tie the various subsidiaries together – not always with great success.

The importance of culture becomes even clearer when looking at cross-border mergers and acquisitions and at the consequent implications in terms of integrating cultures without losing authenticity. Let us return to the case of Carlsberg. In 2008, Carlsberg acquired Baltika, the leader in the Russian beer market. How likely was it that the two cultures would truly merge? In addition, in such a case, would a common culture be useful?

The post-merger integration challenge that Carlsberg faced after the formal approval of the acquisition was enormous.[23] The building of a group culture was defined as a key strategic priority for Carlsberg as early as 2002, long before the acquisition of Baltika. A main concern at that time was that the CEO, Ulrik Andersen, had been struggling to promote alignment across the traditionally strong local units, guided by his belief that 'local is king'. At a large-scale top management strategy workshop held in 2002, many local CEOs voiced their concerns about the 'looseness' of the organization, which they did not believe provided enough common ground. Andersen was taken aback by the group's criticisms of the lack of clear guidance and advice from headquarters, and by the suggestion that communication and collaboration between headquarters and local units were lacking. The local executives asked headquarters to take on a more involved role and to ensure more sharing of best practices, and they sent a clear signal that they wished to become part of a unified company.

---

[23] Hoenen, A.K. and Venzin, M. (2013) Transforming Carlsberg into a Cosmopolitan Firm: Building Strategy Process Capabilities, Cranfield: The Case Centre.

In an attempt to live up to this goal of unifying the company under a common group umbrella, 120 senior executives came together at the IMD business school in Lausanne to engage in interactive sessions. There they agreed on a new mission and four core values, which were subsequently introduced in 2003. In 2006, an internal strategic initiative was launched to infuse the organization with Carlsberg's core values. The initiative to establish 'a winning Carlsberg group culture' was designed to get all employees worldwide on board, and to ensure a shared understanding of Carlsberg's mission and values. Carlsberg's strong traditions and Danish heritage naturally meant that the company culture was dominated by a Scandinavian mindset. Although not explicitly spelled out, Carlsberg was characterized by its own social fabric or 'internal DNA'. Honesty, openness and transparency were held high in the tradition of what it meant to be a 'good' Dane. Carlsberg's 160 years of history highlighted the fact that patience and comfort were also highly valued – there was simply no need to rush to get things done. In general, Carlsberg seemed to display a high level of tolerance and people took the time to listen. Still, Carlsberg was a non-rigid organization that could embrace challenges.

In 2008, the challenge was to integrate the newly acquired Scottish and Newcastle businesses with Carlsberg's existing company culture. Many employees in the acquired units were sceptical about Carlsberg as the new owner. For example, while speaking at the 2008 St. Petersburg Global Management Conference, Anton Artemiev, president of Baltika, turned his back on the audience, pointed at the world map that was displayed on the screen and said: 'Look, this is Russia. This is where we go to bed in the evening and get up to go to work in the morning. And this here – is Denmark.' He did not need to say more. The team handling the Winning Culture post-merger cultural integration project faced a major task. Baltika had enjoyed successful growth in its enormous home market. In 2007, the year prior to the acquisition, Baltika operated eleven breweries with an annual production of 45 million hectolitres and it had over 12,000 employees. Naturally, the company had its own heritage, strategic mission and vision, as well as its own corporate culture and values. For instance, Baltika was accustomed to a rather hierarchical top-down management style, and reward and recognition were highly valued. It was a proud organization.

In attempting to carefully integrate the two cultures, Carlsberg did not try to 'teach' Baltika the Carlsberg values. Instead, it set up a joint project team staffed with twenty-five people from the business side, as well as representatives from HR and group communications across the three regions and across organizational levels. The objective was to map the status quo of existing

values across the geographically dispersed Carlsberg companies by bringing together people from the 'old' pre-acquisition members of the group in
Western Europe and Asia, and from the newly acquired businesses. However,
it quickly became clear that not even the 'old' Carlsberg companies shared a
set of common values. Each local subsidiary representative seemed to be fighting for his or her own local company values. The main problem was that the
corporate values, which had been defined in 2003, had not been efficiently
diffused throughout the organization, and they were interpreted very differently across markets. Therefore, many companies held onto their own value
sets and the project team found it difficult to move forward.

After acknowledging that they could not achieve consensus on a common set
of values, the project team decided to start from scratch at the organizational
base level. The team members agreed that they needed a new concept that
had a cross-cultural focus; was more concrete, descriptive and action-oriented
than abstract values; and clearly described what to do and what not to do.
Thus, they focused their discussions on the behaviours that should guide the
way people worked in the Carlsberg group. The ensuing development process
was surprisingly smooth, as the project team was broken into smaller working groups, each embracing employees from the 'old' Carlsberg companies
and from the newly acquired units, including the Russian organization. The
diverse subgroups had various perspectives but, in the end, they agreed quite
quickly. A set of five 'Winning Behaviours' (WBs) was defined and graphically
illustrated:

1   We place our consumers' and customers' needs at the heart of every
    decision we make.
2   Together we are stronger.
3   We are each empowered to make a difference.
4   We are engaged with society.
5   We want to win.

The WBs concept replaced the former value set and, most importantly, it
reflected the 'new' Carlsberg. The WBs had been developed with the active
involvement of all kinds of people from across the organization. Even the
company's top management team had taken an active role in the process
when it replaced the project team's proposal of 'We should respect diversity'
with 'Together we are stronger', which was a strong signal about the importance of working and growing together. The WBs were designed to be more
action oriented than value oriented in order to convey the shared focus across
cultures.

The new concept was verified with all of the local markets' top management teams at the St. Petersburg Global Management Conference in August 2008. At this meeting, more than 200 top leaders came together and spent an entire day discussing, internalizing and acting out the WBs to enable role modelling. At the Conference, the WBs were on display and everyone present signed them. The former Chief Executive Jørgen Buhl Rasmussen presented an ambitious guideline for implementation – the WBs were to be implemented throughout the group as soon as possible and replace the existing values no later than September 2009. Rasmussen stated: 'The Winning Behaviours hold one of the keys to the success of our Group. I believe that the Winning Behaviours will be the foundation for the way we want to do things and how we develop a shared culture across the Group. The Winning Behaviours differentiate us from our competitors, they are the people and organisational "glue", and they are critical for our success and growth.'[24]

The WBs and the roll-out process were in line with Carlsberg's 'glocal approach' to managing the multinational, multicultural group. The roll-out and cascading of the WBs into the organization was not simply a top-down directive or a headquarters campaign – different organizational levels and cross-functional teams were actively involved. Three aspects were viewed as particularly critical for the roll-out's success.

First, the WBs would need to be effectively linked with strategy. In other words, the behaviours had to be well anchored, from the strategy level down, in the day-to-day operations. People at all levels would need to understand how adopting the WBs would help them to implement Carlsberg's strategy, and achieve their targets and goals.

Second, processes across the organization needed to be aligned to explicitly support the behaviours. Key management systems, such as performance management, leadership development and communication tools, needed to be redesigned to encourage people to adopt the WBs. The project team therefore developed a toolkit to support the roll-out across the group and to establish links to existing processes (such as leadership development programmes, 360° feedback, employee-attitude surveys, performance reviews and recruiting processes).

Third, the organization needed to bring the behaviours to life. In other words, it needed to present them in a way that people recognized as truthful to their experience, and embedded in the organizational history and narrative. Storytelling was used as a communication strategy. Real-life

[24] Carlsberg Internal Company Presentation 'From Values to Behaviours', February 2009.

stories were shared about how WBs had been demonstrated by real leaders in real situations to get real results. The guiding principles were to describe the WBs using simple language, and to provide a 'storybook' describing WBs in action across countries and functions. This was done by setting up a unique web portal on the Intranet in which more than 700 selected stories and ideas were collected that everyone in the group could access and 'steal' with pride. This was a simple but impactful and well-received vehicle for sharing WB anecdotes from all levels, from the shop floor to top management, and across regions. The behaviours quickly spread throughout the organization.

As the Carlsberg example shows, the level and speed of cultural integration need to be chosen carefully. Often, identifying a set of values that includes very different cultures is impossible. In such cases, it is better to learn to respect and value differences, and to focus on defining shared procedures and ways to approach business issues. Consider, for example, Renault-Nissan. Linked by cross-shareholdings – Renault owns 44.4 per cent of Nissan and Nissan owns 15 per cent of Renault – these two companies share a coherent strategy, common objectives and principles, industrial cooperation and trade, but they respect their identities and brands. There are limits to 'stretching' culture for companies as well as individuals.

In this regard, Fabrizio Longo, managing director of Hyundai Italia, states: 'There is a marked dialectic between the Korean culture, characterized by a strong work ethic and a sense of diligence, and the European culture. The European management has a good share of responsibility in the local governance of decisions and local tastes are taken into account, but the Korean matrix remains strong.' Fabrizio Finzi, the dealer network development director of Hyundai Italia, comments: 'We maintain the better of two opposing views. There is a strong oligarchic structure whereby decisions are made in Korea but considerable voice is also given to the markets. How? With a strong presence of local Korean staff in the company. It is not only a system of control, but also a way of bringing ideas and challenges to the top management.'

A strong imprinting of national values that can be exported abroad, as in the case of Nestlé or Volkswagen, sometimes increases organizational resilience. However, in the case of very different cultures, flanking rather than superimposing increases organizational resilience. It is often more effective to work on shared 'winning' behaviours that are closely tied to strategy and objectives than on imposing common values on a set of culturally diverse subsidiaries.

HOW AUTHENTIC IS YOUR FIRM?

Our research suggests that high authenticity increases resilience and, in turn, produces SSP. To assess the level of a firm's authenticity, we have developed a quick test. This instrument allows managers to diagnose the current situation and uncovers relevant future actions. The various factors can be evaluated on a scale from 1 to 5 (where 1 = strongly disagree and 5 = completely agree) and are linked to resilience-related actions that can be introduced in the company. You are free to modify the tool and integrate the short questionnaire with other items or indicators that are already used to measure performance in various areas of the firm.

Table 3.1 Assess your firm's authenticity

	Strongly disagree ⟵————⟶ Completely agree				
	1	2	3	4	5
My values are similar or identical to those of my organization.					
My organization is rooted in solid values over time and not in short-term goals.					
The promises that my organization makes to consumers are in line with its values.					
My organization remains true to itself and is recognizable by its consumers even in times of crisis.					
Authenticity score (the average of the four answers)					
Reference grid *	1–2: Low resilience. Your company is not prepared for external shocks and needs to invest in a resilience programme.				
	3: Average resilience. Identify blind resilience spots and work on them.				
	4–5: High resilience. Stay the course. Make sure you remain on alert.				

Source: Adapted from Eggers et al. (2013).

* If the average of the responses from each chapter in this book is between 1 and 2, then the organization's approach to resilience is weak. If the average is 3, the company is at an intermediate stage and needs to invest in resilience. If the average of the responses is between 4 and 5, the organization is on track to achieving positive and stable results over time.

CHAPTER 4

Customer Centricity

In 2012, Diego Della Valle, owner of Tod's, used a newspaper article to provoke the Fiat CEO, saying: 'The real problem with Fiat is not the workers, Italy or the crisis (which certainly exists). The real problem is its shareholders and chief executive. They are the ones who are making the wrong decisions. If the customer is happy, sooner or later the shareholders will also be.' (*Corriere della Sera*, 14 September 2012).[1]

Companies are returning to the consumer perspective. As Sam Walton, founder of Walmart, says: 'there is only one boss, the customer. He can dismiss everyone, from the CEO downwards, simply by choosing to spend his money somewhere else'. This statement gives a good idea of how important it is to be centred on the customer – to be 'customer centric'.

A focus on customers requires 'falling in love with the product'. Giovanni Rana, an innovative fresh-pasta producer, is one example. He puts his products above all other interests. His goal is to communicate the quality of his pasta, which is industrial in form but artisan in terms of its production mechanisms. His products are characterized by true quality that captures the desires and needs of consumers, and by constant innovation. The first rule, according to Rana, is to be in love with your work and the product that is produced without ever forgetting where you came from. The second rule is authenticity – genuineness in standing behind the product, and the desire to look into the customer's eyes to assure them that what you are selling is exactly as you are describing it. Thus, the only competition that the Verona-based entrepreneur fears is 'the grandmother with a rolling pin' (*Castellanzaonline*, 19 March 2012).[2]

---

[1] The interview 'Della Valle all'attacco: Il vero problema della Fiat? Il suo amministratore delegato' is available at: www.corriere.it/economia/12_settembre_14/dellavalle-marchionne -fiat_4470aa88-fe90-11e1-82d3-7cd1971272b9.shtml.

[2] See 'L'unica concorrenza che temo è la nonna col mattarello' at: www.castellanzaonline.it/ news/4/376/.

In the same way, the contemporary master-craft enterprises mentioned in Chapter 3 owe their success and their ability to withstand the recent crisis to their focus on customer needs, as well as their attention to detail in terms of quality, authenticity and connections to traditions and the territory. Moreover, they show true love for the product. In today's context, this model succeeds because it leads companies out of the global competition by ensuring a competitive advantage that is difficult to imitate.

Along these lines, the Swiss fine-biscuit company Kambly, which was founded in 1910, puts tradition, product quality and customer experience at the centre of its strategy. The family firm's CEO, Oscar A. Kambly, states: 'Perhaps the reason so many people have been satisfied with our quality for so many years is that we never will be.' The obsession with product quality and customer delight has made Kambly an internationally recognized brand. 'Authenticity' and 'origin' are important concepts for the company:

> Kambly has been baking speciality biscuits in the heart of Switzerland for some 100 years, day in, day out, with the same dedication. Here in the Emmental valley, home to fresh milk and butter, the quality of life is tangible. The majority of raw ingredients come from local suppliers – flour from the local mill, butter from the local dairy. Over 80% of Kambly's raw ingredients either come from Switzerland or are processed here – chocolate, for example, is produced to Kambly's own recipe by renowned Swiss chocolate manufacturers.[3]

Customer orientation leads to superior products and services that have to be protected. In Geox, a leading company in the production of shoes, many of the products derive from patents. In 1995, when Geox began industrial production, it filed a patent for a perforated rubber sole. As a testimony to its love for its products, Geox now has sixty patents registered in Italy. Technically, being in love with the product means introducing a business strategy that leverages consumer needs, and knowing how to formulate the next steps in terms of marketing, merchandising and operations so that they are aligned with the priorities of consumers (Ross, 2009). Customer-centric firms try to measure how well they meet customers' needs. To determine whether a customer-centric strategy is in place, at least five relevant quantitative parameters can be used: the number of new customers, the number of customers who leave (customer retention), the number of products that the customer uses

---

[3] www.kambly.com/en/691/Quality-policy.htm.

(products per household), customer satisfaction and the number of customers who would recommend the company to others (Gummesson, 2008).

FROM TOTAL SHAREHOLDER RETURN TO CUSTOMER CENTRICITY

There have been at least two major trends in modern capitalism. The first, which emerged in the 1930s, highlighted the importance of managers. The second shifted the focus towards the importance of shareholders. This second wave, which began in the late 1970s, continues today. For example, the main objectives of the major investment banks are making money and pleasing shareholders. Those who work on Wall Street earn astronomical sums (Martin, 2010).

However, two of our time's greatest business figures – Roberto Goizueta, CEO of Coca-Cola from 1981 until his death in 1997, and Jack Welch, CEO of General Electric from 1981 to 2001 – after first maintaining the importance of shareholders began to question that view. Towards the end of his career in 2009, Jack Welch stated: 'On the face of it, shareholder value is the dumbest idea in the world. Shareholder value is a result, not a strategy. Your main constituencies are your employees, your customers and your products. Managers and investors should not set share price increases as their overarching goal ... Short-term profits should be allied with an increase in the long-term value of a company.'[4]

With the tragic events of 2008, which included the Wall Street crisis, we see this paradigm enter into the picture. The fundamental assumption radically changed – the shareholder is no longer at the centre and the path to profit ends without leading to good results in the long run.

The organizational structures of companies were once designed with the customer as the last step in the production chain. Today's structure, in which the customer is at the centre of the firm's organizational machine, is defined 'outside-in' (Towers, 2010). There have been many cases in recent times of 'co-designing' products with customers. Volkswagen China, for example, carried out a contest to design a new car for the people.

The transition is not purely theoretical. It involves concrete actions to move in the direction of the consumer. To increase resilience, business processes, choices and strategic decisions must all be oriented towards customer

---

[4] See 'The dumbest idea in the world: maximizing shareholder value' at: www.forbes.com/sites/stevedenning/2011/11/28/maximizing-shareholder-value-the-dumbest-idea-in-the-world/2/.

centricity. For an airline, activities traditionally began with the sale of tickets and ended with the delivery of luggage after the flight. At Southwest Airlines – one of the few US airlines that has been able to maintain its profits in times of crisis – the process is structured differently. The start of operations begins when the customer starts thinking about needing a flight and ends when he returns home (Towers, 2010). Southwest claims to be in the 'business of moving people'.

Our research indicates that more resilient companies are those that are able to focus on customers and their needs, especially in times of crisis. This is the case for Hyundai, which designed the 'Hyundai Assurance' programme for the American market following the 2008 crisis. The programme allowed customers to return a car for up to a year if they became unemployed or were economically affected by the crisis. Another example is found in Audi, which developed the 'Audi Experience', a programme in which managers of all divisions visited the brand's main customers to ask them about their needs. Similarly, Apple is obsessed with its customers. Steve Jobs was not primarily interested in whether a product produced revenue but rather in making a good product that would please – or even surprise – customers. Many successful companies in the digital world also focus on the customer experience. At the heart of Google's philosophy is a focus on customers; everything else is secondary.

The question is then whether the most customer-centric firms are also the ones that are most appreciated by customers. A survey carried out in 2013 by the German Quality and Finance Institute[5] posed two simple questions to 74,275 people. The aim was to evaluate consumer approval of a sample of 274 Italian companies in forty-nine sectors. The questions were the following: 'In the last 36 months, have you been or are you still a customer of one of the following companies/brands?' and 'Have you received very good service from this company?' These questions addressed the customer's emotional experience with the service rather than the company's actual offering. Of the 274 companies included in the survey, ninety-one won gold (i.e. more than 75% of customers received 'very good' service), thirty-six won silver (70–74.9%) and thirty-eight won bronze (65–69.9%). At the top was Amazon, with a rating of 91 per cent, followed by Calzedonia and Booking.com. Not surprisingly, among those at the top of the list in terms of consumer preferences are companies that have turned their efforts towards a customer-centric approach.

[5] See 'Campioni del Servizio. Il più Grande Studio sul servizio in Italia" at: www.istituto-qualita .com/italiano/campioni-del-servizio/.

For example, to guarantee a fast time to market and ensure that customers are not disappointed, each Amazon warehouse worker carries a scanner. The schedule must be respected or the scanner displays a message that tells them to pick up their speed. After five mistakes, a worker is reprimanded. Despite recent scandals, employees say they are satisfied: 80 per cent are permanent staff. The highest priority is to not make customers wait. Amazon equals Walmart in the use of monitoring technologies to track the minute-by-minute movements and performance of its employees. These technologies are used in settings that go beyond the assembly line to include movements between loading and unloading docks, between packing and unpacking stations, and to and from the miles of shelving at what Amazon calls its 'fulfilment centres' – gigantic warehouses to which goods ordered by Amazon's customers are sent by manufacturers and wholesalers, where they are shelved, packaged and sent out again to Amazon customers. 'Ours is a race against time, and I have an obsession with the customer', says Amazon CEO, Jeff Bezos (Forbes, 4 April 2012).[6] More than a century ago, another legendary retailer, Chicago's Marshall Field, championed the fatalist slogan 'The customer is always right'. Perhaps more than anyone, Bezos has taken that mantra into the digital era, incrementally cracking one of the greatest business mysteries: figuring out what customers want before the cash register rings and then making those insights pay off.

The survey placed Calzedonia third in the satisfaction ratings. Calzedonia sells lingerie, stockings and swimsuits through its Calzedonia, Intimissimi and Tezenis brands. It has over EUR 1.5 billion in annual revenue, which is generated in more than thirty countries. It is entering new markets, especially in Asia, starting with Hong Kong. In 1986, the founder, Sandro Veronesi, introduced a new format: a shop with a huge assortment of all types of socks for all ages and tastes. The fundamental idea was based on the insight that a large number of customers were not happy with the product offerings they found in traditional stores. Given that dissatisfaction, Calzedonia allows customers to find all possible variants of a single product, which gives everyone an opportunity to 'customize' the offering with respect to individual tastes and personal preferences. The formula continues unchanged, but other product categories have been added: bathing costumes, lingerie and pyjamas. After a little over twenty-five years, the Calzedonia network boasts more than 1,470 stores around the world and can be said to be absolutely resilient.[7]

---

[6] See 'Jeff Bezos reveals his no. 1 leadership secret' at: www.forbes.com/forbes/2012/0423/ceo -compensation-12-amazon-technology-jeff-bezos-gets-it.html.

[7] To learn more, see 'Veronesi: Calzedonia oltre quota 1,5 miliardi aprirà 400 negozi nel 2013,' 19 April 2013, at: www.moda24.ilsole24ore.com/art/industria-finanza/2013-04-18/veronesi -calzedonia-oltre-quota-132223.php?uuid=AbiQTOoH.

Of course, we can also find examples of the opposite. One online retailer in Switzerland sells only black socks to men who do not want to spend time and effort bygoing to shops to buy socks, and who do not want a colour other than black. In either case, the ability to segment the market and understand customer needs is essential.

In essence, the above examples illustrate that customer centricity refers to:

★ *Love for the product*: customers have sophisticated needs that require greater customization. At the same time, they expect to interact with products that are easy to understand and use.

★ *Excellent processes* that allow the customer to be reached ever more efficiently.

★ *Innovation choices* aimed at anticipating, analysing and satisfying the needs of a well-targeted set of clients.

LOVE FOR THE PRODUCT

In 2012, Luca Cordero di Montezemolo, president of Ferrari until 2014, met Apple's CEO, Tim Cook. The Ferrari chairman was going to speak in front of thousands of students at Stanford University at the View From the Top conference. He demonstrated his alignment with Steve Jobs by asserting: 'We make cars, they make computers. But Apple and Ferrari are bound by the same passion, the same love for the product; maniacal attention to technology but also to design.'[8] Similarly, Ferrero's website includes the statement: 'Since our beginnings as a small town family entrepreneurial business, we have built our success on strong values, pride in our products, and a passion for quality.' Ferrero's Nutella, which is made from Piedmont hazelnuts, first conquered Italy and then international markets. Each ingredient is chosen based on high-quality standards.

When attention to detail is high and the quality that emerges is better than average, consumers are more likely to have a positive perception of the product, and it should win their favour. Love for the product, in other words, can be useful to satisfy a need. Customization and simplification paths can be followed to make the product immediately desirable in the eyes of consumers, and know-how about responding to their needs can be utilized. As mentioned above, this is the approach adopted by the high-end companies operating in Italy, which continued to post impressive results even during the crisis.

[8] See 'Montezemolo come Steve Jobs dice agli studenti di Stanford: "Siate creativi"' at: www .omniauto.it/magazine/19560/montezemolo-come-steve-jobs-dice-agli-studenti-di-standford -siate-creativi.

Customization

The ability to 'customize' a product, or to give consumers the opportunity to configure a product according to their preferences (i.e. being able to choose and formulate a number of options or simplifications), lies at the heart of customer centricity. Sky Television knows this. It has revolutionized television production by creating new models of enjoyment for the consumer. Television products – films, series and documentaries – are shown at various times according to a schedule that includes the same programmes several times a day. This allows customers to watch the programmes they like according at the times that best suit them. Customer centricity has been further enhanced with the MySky HD, a device that allows customers to record a favourite programme, stop it at any time or rewind it if they want to watch a scene again. The choice is in the hands of the consumer.

Nike, the sportswear brand famous for its trainers, has posted excellent performance in recent years. The company allows consumers to create the shoes they want by selecting the colour, shape and fit. Customization choices enable the company to discern customer tastes and to segment customers into various groups for subsequent targeted promotions.

B2B businesses often collaborate in this sense. This is the case for Fainplast, a company specializing in a chemical compound consisting of two or more elements, which posted turnover of EUR 86 million in 2012. The president and founder of Fainplast, Battista Farinotti, put it this way: 'For many customers, including Prysmian and Nexans, we are true partners. We develop products together and provide the necessary assistance. Currently, for example, we are testing a product that will replace rubber for certain applications with savings for customers in the cable industry' (*La Repubblica*, 22 September 2014)[9].

Simplification

Customer centricity often means offering the consumer a product that can be easily understood and just as easily used, especially when it comes to technical firms, specialist products or products that are difficult to understand. In such cases, the best path is following simplification.

For example, banks used to offer customers a broad range of products with complex names that could be confusing. This strategy had an undesired effect,

[9] See 'Plastiche: la formula di Fainplast' at: www.repubblica.it/economia/affari-e-finanza/2014/09/22/news/plastiche_la_formula_di_fainplast_ricerca_logistica_e_investimenti-96368282/.

as it made it difficult for customers to make a choice from among the various options. It thereby disoriented customers – and sometimes even sales representatives in the retail outlets. Banks are now trying to simplify their offerings by including products that are more comprehensible. In line with the simplification trend, Banca Mediolanum came up with a new service called Send Money, which allows customers to transfer money using the Mediolanum mobile application without having to know the beneficiary's IBAN. No complicated code needs to be inserted – an email address or phone number is enough. If the recipient is already a PayPal user, he or she receives the funds instantly.

In terms of combining customization and simplification, the Extrabanca case offers an example of segmenting the market, analysing the needs of target segments and creating specific services for those groups of customers. Extrabanca is an Italian credit institution that aims to serve foreign nationals residing in Italy and the businesses they manage. Extrabanca believes it is unique in its business, as it is not only a credit institution but also a service company, a centre for cultural encounters and an enterprise. Extrabanca's objective is to achieve two separate but complementary results: an increase in profits and recognition as a lever of social integration.

Extrabanca has created an innovative way of offering banking services based on four pillars: welcoming, counselling, simplicity and accessibility. 'Welcoming' means that the customer should feel at ease, and never be intimidated or discriminated against by the bank. In this respect, Extrabanca is a bank without barriers, designed to promote contact between customers and staff. Many of its employees are foreign. In fact, around 50 per cent are from different countries and ethnic groups. As a result, they are not only able to make customers feel at ease, but they can also communicate in the customer's own language.

'Counselling' means creating a dialogue with the customer. Employees are encouraged to give customers all the time they need. In addition, the ability to communicate with customers in their native language facilitates the development of open and transparent communication, which in turn instils confidence. Dialogue also serves to inform customers, who generally have limited financial knowledge. Extrabanca's top management views the time needed to build a relationship with the customer as an investment rather than a cost.

'Simplicity' means offering a limited number of products that the customer is able to understand. Some examples are Extra@home, a loan enabling foreigners to buy a home in their country of origin, and Extramoneytransfer, which allows customers to transfer money quickly for a very low fee.

'Accessibility' means facilitating interaction between customers and the bank. Extrabanca has unusually long opening hours, from 9.00 a.m. to 7.00 p.m., including Saturdays, and it is sometimes also open on Sundays. The weekends are often dedicated to a particular ethnic group or theme. Accessibility also means that all branches are located in safe areas, but not areas that are too prestigious, so as to avoid intimidating the customer. These are usually areas with a high proportion of foreigners. The company's motto is 'We are always open'.

EXCELLENT PROCESSES

Increased efficiency in internal processes enables information on current and potential customers to be gathered and organized. It also ensures quick responses aimed at meeting the needs of identified targets.

Passion for the product is not enough. For example, the efficiency of production processes and technology investments are the basis of ASICS's strategy. The company's research institute in Kobe, around 200 miles west of Tokyo, contains more than 45,000 square feet of research facilities. Several test rooms are part of the complex. The observation and analysis of physical movements is the foundation of every ASICS product. The researchers in Kobe have high-speed cameras, hi-tech measuring equipment and sophisticated computer software at their disposal. Every ASICS innovation idea is intended to create the best product and to meet the customer's needs. This includes integrating the industrial processes that regulate and accelerate the complex footwear and sportswear production chain. Similarly, Gordon Ramsey, the famous Michelin-starred chef, said: 'Cooking is a passion, but you also have to be very practical. I have opened 21 restaurants in the world and I know that if things don't work in the kitchen, the customer can't be served and will never return. The machine must run' (*The Guardian*, 19 October 2013).[10]

There is also a growing tendency towards increasing interactions between customers and companies by providing customers with access to call centres, toll-free numbers, dedicated email addresses and physical branches open 24 hours a day, all of which are ready to respond to different requests. Barclays, for example, began 2001 with the development of a network-service model for its customers. The bank began to gradually extend the opening hours in its main branches to 8.00 p.m. and it opened some branches on Saturdays.

[10] See 'Gordon Ramsay: "I'm still excited by perfection"' at: www.theguardian.com /lifeandstyle/2013/oct/19/gordon-ramsay-still-excited-by-perfection.

Barclay's CEO, Matt Barrett, said: 'The old reality of bankers' hours doesn't cut it anymore. We are therefore delighted to offer our customers the opportunity to visit branches outside the usual times' (Money Marketing, 27 April 2001).[11]

Unicredit is launching a pilot project in Sofia, Bulgaria, in which the 'branch of the future' is being tested. Innovative solutions are offered for each interaction phase: (1) capture attention from outside (e.g. large transparent glass walls and exterior communication screens); (2) enter the branch (e.g. introduction of customer managers, self-service areas, queue-management system); (3) orientation (e.g. creation of a 'fast-service zone' at the heart of the branch); (4) waiting (e.g. free Wi-Fi, refreshments, information screens); (5) interaction with the bank (e.g. remote video consultations with experts from central offices); and (6) departure (e.g. immediate feedback system). Our study has identified several cases of resilient firms that experiment with innovative process solutions in well-confined areas (often within the periphery of their operations) first. This leads us to the third frontier of customer centricity: innovation.

INNOVATION

Innovation is an approach that anticipates needs or creates new ones. For instance, in addition to his love for his product, Giovanni Rana has continuously invested in innovation. In 1966, his pasta factory had good turnover, but he could not sell his products in the surrounding areas because the tortellini had a maximum shelf life of three days. Following the principle that sparkling water lasts longer than natural water because it contains carbon dioxide, Giovanni Rana wondered whether introducing carbon dioxide into the tortellini vacuum packs would help the tortellini last longer. His intuition became a reality – fresh tortellini went from lasting three days to fifteen days. The potential market immediately expanded beyond central Italy. Some years later, the introduction of a new technology, known as modified atmosphere packaging, allowed Rana's company to achieve longer storage and sale times, and to reach more distant markets.

To be resilient, a firm must be able to anticipate and interpret the needs of consumers, and even invent new needs. Apple, with the launch of the iPad and iPhone, responded to needs that consumers did not even know they had. We find similar examples in history. Henry Ford famously said: 'If I had asked my customers what they wanted, they would have said "a faster horse".' In Ford's

[11] See 'Barclays to extend the opening hours' at: www.moneymarketing.co.uk/barclays-to -extend-opening-hours/69112.article.

time, customers probably did not know that they wanted a car, just as more modern consumers were not aware that they needed a smartphone. Similarly, although market research had shown that customers would not want to see a transparent container filled with dust on a vacuum cleaner, James Dyson, founder of Dyson, decided to produce it anyway. The transparent container became one of the distinctive features of the vacuum cleaners produced by the company, and it was a huge sales success. For Dyson, asking customers what they wanted early in the innovation process would have limited innovation. Of course, this does not mean that companies should ignore customer needs. Rather, they should recognize that sometimes customers do not know what they really want. Would you have told James Dyson that you wanted to see the dirt your vacuum cleaner extracted from your carpets? Probably not. However, this is now one of the features that customers appreciate the most.

As Figure 4.1 shows, resilient firms not only look for product and service innovations, but they also aim to improve their production processes in order to obtain benefits in the form of lower costs and differentiation advantages. HeidelbergCement, for example, used to focus its innovation efforts on the bottom-left quadrant of Figure 4.1 on the basis of the assumption that cost advantages could be gained by modifying production processes. However, a group-wide innovation contest triggered over one hundred ideas, and showed that it was possible to escape the commodity trap in the cement business.

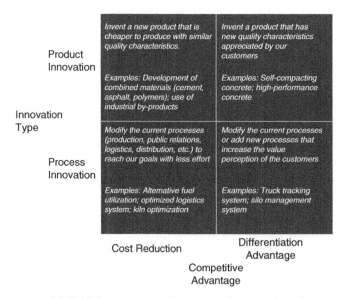

Figure 4.1 HeidelbergCement's "innovation/competitive advantage matrix"
Source: authors' own based on HeidelbergCement data

COMMODITIES DO NOT EXIST

Customer centricity is essential not only in fast-moving consumer goods sectors but also in industries that sell more standardized products, such as basic energy cables, cement or sugar. Any kind of business, even the most standardized, can always be differentiated according to customer needs. Think about a contract for standardized products. Each clause in the contract can be a point for differentiation – perhaps in terms of delivery times, packaging or product features. Each business always has a service component that can be exploited and improved. Gioacchino De Chirico, past CEO of Immucor, a company specializing in transfusion medicine, said: 'Our business is rather technical. Some might even call it a commodity. In reality, there are no businesses that are commodities. I take any business and differentiate it, try to improve it, add a service component so the customer remains satisfied. We want to be the best in dialysis and the customer notices this.' The financial results speak for themselves. Immucor has achieved outstanding performance over the past decade. From a loss of USD 50 million in 2001, Immucor achieved sales of around USD 240 million and an operating income of more than USD 110 million in 2007. In 2008, *The Wall Street Journal* listed Immucor at number four (right behind Apple) on its list of ten-year best performers in terms of shareholder return, with 40.5 per cent.

How was this turnaround possible? The key ingredients in a turnaround success story are simple to list but hard to execute:

1 Cultural change: do not allow anyone in your organization, especially your sales people, to view your product as a commodity.
2 Market segmentation: do not treat your customers as one homogeneous group of people looking for low prices.
3 Customer intimacy: invest time in understanding your customers' businesses.
4 Innovation and scale: work on innovative ideas in every organizational process in order to cater to customers' needs. Consolidate your industry to get the necessary market power to introduce your innovative ideas.
5 Measure success: get everyone motivated and aligned by introducing a sophisticated performance-measurement system.

The cement business can be described as a mature market with diminishing opportunities for the development of competitive advantage. Nevertheless, global cement producers are trying to achieve stable price premiums by increasing service levels, as indicated in Figure 4.2.

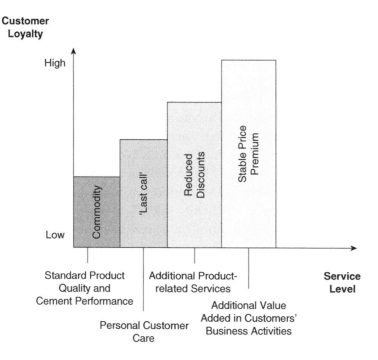

Figure 4.2 HeidelbergCement's "stairway to a stable price premium"
Source: authors' own based on HeidelbergCement data

To be viewed as a supplier, cement producers have to be able to deliver cement of a given quality. Customer loyalty is low, and most contracts are awarded to the cement producer that offers its products at the lowest price. However, through personal customer care, cement producers may become the 'preferred' supplier if they match competitors' prices after they receive a 'last call' for quotations. Reduced discounts can be achieved through additional product-related services, such as automatized management of clients' cement silos or a tracking system that allows customers to control cement deliveries. In some geographical areas, it is even possible to achieve stable price premiums by adding value to customers' business activities that are not directly related to cement. For example, the much larger cement companies can help their small or medium-sized customers improve their logistics processes without charging a fee for such services. Such efforts pay off. Clients are happy to receive free consulting and may, therefore, be more loyal. Moreover, the supply chain interface with customers is optimized according to the cement producers' standards, which reduces costs for cement producers.

HOW CUSTOMER CENTRIC IS YOUR FIRM?

Our research suggests that high customer centricity increases resilience and, in turn, produces sustained superior performance (SSP). To assess the extent to which a firm is customer centric, use this 'quick test' (see Table 4.1). The various factors can be evaluated on a scale from 1 to 5 (where 1 = strongly disagree and 5 = completely agree) and are linked to the resilience-related actions that can be introduced in the company. You are free to modify the tool and integrate the short questionnaire with other items or indicators that are already used to measure performance in various areas of the firm.

Table 4.1 **Assess your firm's customer centricity**

	Strongly disagree				Completely agree
	1	2	3	4	5
My organization orients its actions to the desires of consumers.					
My organization develops products that are able to meet the expectations of current and potential consumers.					
My organization is able to provide quick responses to customers given the integrated knowledge of consumers it has in its various functions.					
My organization has established clear business goals in connection with acquiring, developing and retaining consumers.					
Customer-centricity score (take the average of the four answers)					
Reference grid	1–2: Low resilience. You need to change your choices and effect a turnaround.				
	3: Average resilience. You need to invest in resilience and adopt a definite direction.				
	4–5: High resilience. Stay the course and emphasize your strengths.				

Source: Adapted from Ata and Toker (2012).

CHAPTER 5

Product Focus

Research on the relationship between product diversification and performance has been the subject of heated debate over the past three decades (Chatterjee and Wernerfelt, 1991; Miller, 2004; Rumelt, 1974). The study of this relationship has been influenced by the resource-based view (RBV). The RBV suggests that the type of diversification that a company can put in place and its performance are conditional on the pool of resources and competencies that the company owns or is capable of generating. The literature suggests that direct diversification which is closely linked to the existing business segments leads to superior performance when compared to enlarged diversification or a strategy centred on a single business (Barney, 1991; Rumelt, 1982; Grant, 1987). The dominant model is the very flat inverted-U model (Palich, Cardinal and Miller, 2000), which suggests that – on average – moderate product diversification is beneficial for performance. Nevertheless, no cohesive view of the relationship between the two variables has yet been reached.

FINDING THE OPTIMUM LEVEL OF DIVERSIFICATION

Our survey of the banking industry shows a specific relationship between diversification and resilience. We measured product diversification in terms of the number of different markets and the contributions of those markets to total sales. In this regard, we followed Hoskisson et al. (1993), who tested the validity of 'entropy' as a measure of diversification. This measure, which uses SIC codes and sales for each segment, sums up direct diversification in segments closely related to the company, as well as indirect, or enlarged, diversification with respect to those segments. We find that the more resilient companies are those that simplify the structure of their businesses and remain focused on their core competencies.

Core competencies are defined as 'areas of expertise on which companies decide to focus' (Prahalad and Hamel, 1990, p. 81). They are the building blocks that allow a company to compete better than its rivals (Frery, 2006). In this regard, product focus can be very powerful. The film *300* tells the story of Leonidas, King of Sparta in ancient Greece, who pitted fierce resistance against the Persian army at the pass of Thermopylae during the second Persian war. The event offers a good representation of the concept of core competencies. Leonidas' army was composed of only 300 men, all of whom were soldiers trained for war. Their number was small, but their specialization was such that it enabled great achievements in war.

> DAXOS (COMMANDER OF ARCADIA): I see I was wrong to expect Sparta's commitment to at least match our own.
> KING LEONIDAS: Doesn't it?
> [Points to Arcadian soldier behind Daxos]
> KING LEONIDAS: You there! What is your profession?
> FREE GREEK-POTTER: I am a potter, sir.
> KING LEONIDAS: [points to another soldier] And you, Arcadian! What is your profession?
> FREE GREEK-SCULPTOR: Sculptor, sir.
> KING LEONIDAS: Sculptor.
> [Turns to a third soldier]
> KING LEONIDAS: You?
> FREE GREEK-BLACKSMITH: Blacksmith.
> KING LEONIDAS: [turns back shouting] SPARTANS! What is YOUR profession?
> SPARTANS: WAR! WAR! WAR!
> KING LEONIDAS: [turning to Daxos] You see, old friend? I brought more soldiers than you did!
>
> (Excerpt of a dialogue from the film *300*)

Leonidas and his war specialists forced the Persian army to squeeze into a narrow gorge. The Persians had no choice but to manoeuvre in a narrow space when the battle turned to hand-to-hand combat in which the difference in numbers was no longer an issue. The Roman Empire can also be cited as an example of a focus on core competencies. The Empire focused on a limited, easily defensible area – an unassailable location (Carmeli and Markman, 2011).

In the business world, an example is found in Novo Nordisk, a pharmaceutical company that focuses only on diabetes care and biopharmaceuticals. Its strength lies in the development, expression and formulation of proteins. Another company in the pharmaceutical industry, Chiesi, focuses on very specific areas: respiratory diseases, rare diseases, musculoskeletal disorders and cardiovascular diseases. Both companies have achieved positive and stable performance over time. Similarly, after a period of intense diversification, Enel decommissioned many accessory businesses in order to focus on a simplified energy supply chain: production, distribution and sales. According to its CFO, Luigi Ferraris, this type of simplification 'allows for the replication of the model in overseas markets and uniquely positions the company with respect to its primary abilities. Enel is, above all, a company with engineering-type skills'.

The bottom line is that we cannot really define the optimal level of product diversification. The main message that we want to convey is: 'The optimal level of diversification is lower than you imagine.' There are certainly successful conglomerates, but they are often in emerging countries (e.g. Tata or the Koc Group) or they are companies with very specific operational models. Virgin, for example, is active in sectors ranging from aviation to physical fitness, and brings together more than 200 companies under one brand.

PRODUCT DIVERSIFICATION IN THE CAR INDUSTRY

Those companies that have opted for greater focalization are those that have achieved the highest levels of VOLARE. The automotive sector offers some significant insights in this regard. In comparing companies with high VOLARE (e.g. Porsche and Audi) to those with low VOLARE (e.g. Peugeot and Ford), we find major differences in the choices they made over the past decade. Porsche is resilient with a strong position in a clearly identified luxury niche market and a portfolio consisting of only five products: 911, Boxter, Cayenne, Cayman, Panamera and one car in the very high price range, the coveted 918 Spyder (Figure 5.1).

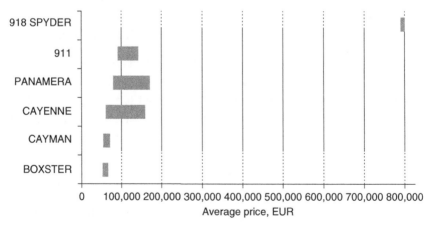

Figure 5.1 Price bands for Porsche models
Source: authors' own

Such an approach can be very risky, as all bets are on a few selected products. However, in absolute terms, the results appear rewarding. In fact, Porsche's VOLARE is as high as BMW's, but Porsche has much higher volatility, which is offset by higher profitability.

The relationship between product diversification and VOLARE can also be explained at the cognitive level. With a broad product portfolio, the margin of error is higher. If one of the many products does not sell well, the other products can make up for the poor performance. A broad product portfolio entails the possibility of making mistakes, which can lead a company to fail to accurately weigh all decisions. When a company has only a few strong products, it knows it cannot afford to make mistakes and has to consider every detail using a cautious and reasoned approach.

Increased awareness and attention to available choices increases the likelihood of identifying the most appropriate strategy. Audi (VOLARE 10) produces a slightly higher number of models, but the price differences between one model and another are substantial. In this way, each car is dedicated to different levels of consumer spending power. The prices range from an average of EUR 17,000 for an A1 to EUR 129,000 for an R8 (Figure 5.2).

The products produced by Audi and Porsche are few and recognizable in the consumer's mind. The situation is very different when analysing the graphs for carmakers with low VOLARE (see Figure 5.3). Peugeot's greatest success was

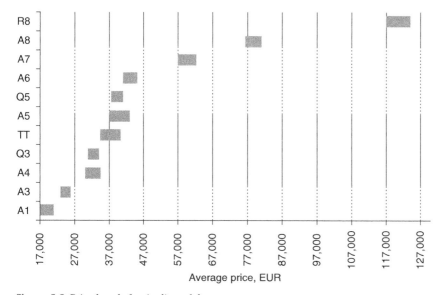

Figure 5.2 Price bands for Audi models
Source: authors' own

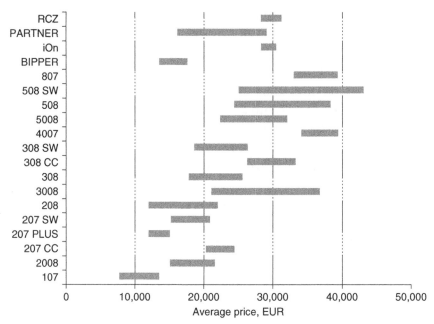

Figure 5.3 Price bands for Peugeot models
Source: authors' own

the Peugeot 205. In January 1983, the press was given the opportunity to test drive the new car. The media was impressed by its agility and exceptional handling. The model was also positively received by the public – the image transmitted was agreeable, fresh and dynamic. The car was an instant hit among the female public, while the sporty versions later gained approval from the male public. The 205 created a 'family feeling'. Moreover, the line was simple but not obvious, and relatively modern for its time. The sport versions were pleasant, likeable and spirited.

In 1998, the production of the Peugeot 206 began, which ended the era of the 205. An attempt was made to replicate the technical features and design that had made the 205 car a perfect mix for consumers, but the same formula was not to be found. Peugeot proceeded by trial and error, and it has launched several new models in the last decade. In the mid-2000s, the PSA Peugeot Citroën Group entered into a joint venture with BMW, from which the Prince engine was born. The engine was mounted on the new Mini and on some mid-low range PSA models. In the same period, the 107 arrived. The car was less sporty and more of a city car than the 106 it replaced. In this period, Peugeot sought new market niches, which were to be occupied by new models with normal production and characterized by larger interior space than conventional models, and by other special technical functionalities and new body configurations. These particular models had two zeros in their names. This is how the first 1007– a small people carrier to counter such cars as the Opel Agila – was born in 2005. Two years later, the 4007 debuted. This was the French manufacturer's first SUV, which was developed through a joint venture with Mitsubishi. In 2009, Peugeot introduced the 3008, a special crossover vehicle that was part SUV, part people carrier and part station wagon.

Peugeot's customers were not satisfied with either the quality or the price of the new vehicles. Peugeot and Citroen were listed at the bottom of European rankings in the various customer and dealer satisfaction indices (*Financial Times*, 11 September 2012)[1]. The designs appeared to lack the flair of the previous models, and the manufacturer's average consumer was part of an increasingly aging target market. Market research undertaken in 2008 showed that the PSA customer was, on average, around 43 years old. Peugeot was perceived as a generalist manufacturer. As such, it was crushed by low-cost producers in Eastern Europe, such as Skoda, and by premium producers in Germany.

Some attempts were made to move towards the premium arena, although the launches of different models were slow and not particularly competitive. The new Peugeot RCZ coupe was introduced, and the company made significant investments in electric cars (Figure 5.3).

Ford (VOLARE 0) offers a few recognizable cars, such as the Ford Focus, that have been sold for years. However, these are exceptions in the complex landscape of all Ford models. In the compact-car segment, Ford could use its Ford Focus to look outside the US market. In Europe, the situation was serious and plants were closing, while the consumption of compact cars was dramatically increasing in India and other emerging markets. Ford therefore had great potential to exploit the situation. Other car manufacturers, such as General Motors, Honda, Toyota and Hyundai, were investing in India, but there seemed to be little room for many producers. Hyundai entered the Indian market a year after Ford but quickly overtook its US competitor to become the second-largest player in the market thanks to its policy of investing in compact cars.

In 2005, in the United States, Ford was forced to withdraw faulty cars from the market at a loss of USD 500 million. Ford reacted to this financial loss with a decision to discharge part of its workforce and stop the production of new models. Ford received 660 reports from the National Highway Traffic

[1] See 'Report highlights Peugeot strategic errors' at: https://app.ft.com/cms/s/604b0f4a-fbfd
 -11e1-af33-00144feabdc0.html.

Safety Administration (NHTSA) of spontaneous car fires. In 2011, the negative trend seemed to begin again, with Ford ranking twenty-third in the JD Power Initial Quality Study, an authoritative study on the perceived quality of cars on the market. In 2010, it had been fifth, above both Honda and Toyota. The 2011 ranking was not only below the Japanese manufacturers but also below Chrysler. The problems were mostly related to technology, although the design was also characterized as not particularly impressive.

In this period, an idea emerged to reintroduce the name of one of the models that had created Ford's success in the past: Taurus. The company hoped the use of 'Taurus' would serve to boost sales and fill the void of desirable cars in the eyes of consumers. In 2007, Ford renamed a model that was not selling well – the Five Hundred – making it the new Taurus. 'This [is] one of the problems that Ford has. With all these name changes, Ford has lost a lot of customers', said Rebecca Lindland, an IHS Global Insight analyst (*The Washington Post*, 6 February 2007)[2] (Figure 5.4).

Fiat is also facing a difficult situation, as 'Planet Fiat is going through a complex time with no new models, and those on the market are increasingly

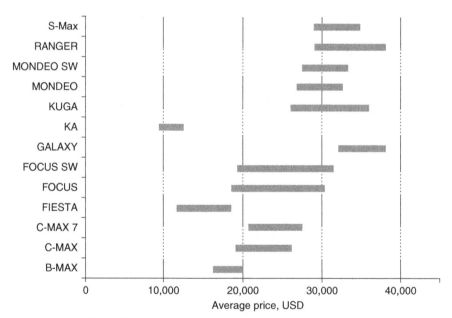

Figure 5.4 Price bands for Ford models
Source: authors' own

[2] See 'Ford Hopes Taurus Name Will Revive Sales' at: www.washingtonpost.com/wp-dyn/content/article/2007/02/06/AR2007020600349_pf.html.

outdated and more expensive than the competition.' (*Corsa News*, 12 July 2012)[3] 'It was once known that Fiat produced the Panda, the Uno and the Punto. This is no longer the case. For example, in recent years, nine car models have disappeared from the Fiat Group catalogue and have not been replaced: from the Croma to the Multipla, from the Idea to the Musa, up to the Alfa 166 (*Panorama*, 24 September 2012)[4] (Figure 5.5).

The production figures for models that currently represent Fiat's flagship offering are highly negative. Several models, including the Fiat Bravo, have not been well received by the market. Initially, Fiat expected to produce around 120,000 cars per year, and early sales were consistent with this forecast. Then sales collapsed, such that the figure is now barely 40,000. Even the results for the Fiat Punto no longer shine through. Despite its position as Fiat's flagship model, this car has undergone a 60 per cent reduction in production over the last ten years. The annual total production estimate for the Punto Classic and the Grande Punto (the more modern version) was initially 600,000, but it has

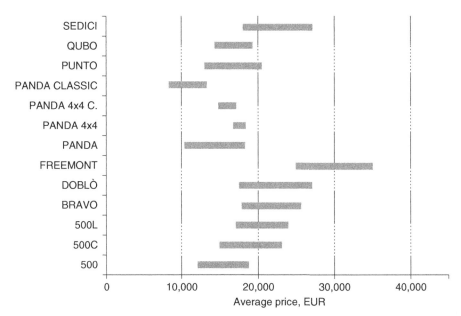

Figure 5.5 Price bands for Fiat models
Source: authors' own

[3] See 'I flop del marketing Fiat: dalla 500 l con caffe'.....alla benzina a 1 euro' at: www.corsanews .it/index.php?option=com_content&view=article&id=6578:i-flop-del-marketing-fiat-dalla-500 -l-con-caffealla-benzina-a-1-euro&catid=9&Itemid=26.
[4] See 'Fiat Panda, Punto, Bravo: tutti i modelli-flop di Marchionne' at: http://economia .panorama.it/panda-punto-bravo-modelli-flop-marchionne.

since been reduced to 260,000 (*Panorama*, 24 September 2012). Fiat is currently focusing more on the Fiat 500. However, the numbers for this product are also poor. The plant in Tychy will produce around 250,000 cars which can be compared to approximately 450,000 produced previously.

The flop of the 500 is reflected in North American sales. In October 2011, 21,380 Fiat 500s were bought, far less than half of the 50,000 forecast. 'We need to work on distribution' admitted Marchionne, who continued: 'In the US, we have 60 Fiat 500 distributors. I believe Ferrari has more' (*La Repubblica*, 18 September 2012)[5]. Fiat also launched the American Fiat 500, which is not 'American' because it is exclusively destined for the US market but because it is blue, a colour that is not in the original 500 range, and has stars and stripes on the wing mirrors and sides. This is a 'limited edition', and every dealer will have one or two units. Apparently, some customers have told dealers: 'I will buy it if you remove those stickers. I care little for the United States, I want it because it is blue – Italy's national colour' (*Corsa News*, 12 July 2012)[6].

Why Do So Many Firms Have Unfocused Product Portfolios?

Many firms pay more attention to adding new products in order to grow than to divesting existing products that do not provide the desired results. Too often, it is (apparently) easier to add another product category than to gain market share in an existing category. Many managers find it hard to turn down creative ideas, so they let colleagues continue to develop them. At some point – without a deliberate, informed decision – the ideas become too big to stop. Resilient firms manage to develop a coherent set of innovative products and services. One way to do so is by using a rather strict product development process with a clear innovation funnel and hard milestones that have to be passed before getting green light for the next development step. However, in many firms, new product ideas mushroom without much of a masterplan. There are too many independent actors – business-unit managers, strategy directors, R & D heads, and commercial directors – who push for product innovation. There is nothing wrong with innovation, but it has to be orchestrated.

Let us consider an extreme example of a network of independent actors engaged in innovation: the mountain resort of St. Moritz, which has been

---

[5] See 'Marchionne: "Manterrò Fiat in Italia con i guadagni fatti all'estero' at: www.repubblica.it /economia/2012/09/18/news/fiat_intervista_marchionne-42748612/.

[6] See 'I flop del marketing Fiat' at: http://corsanews.it/index.php?option=com _content&view=article&id=6578:i-flop-del-marketing-fiat-dalla-500-l-con-caffealla-benzina-a-1 -euro&catid=9&Itemid=26.

known for its outstanding results in the Swiss tourism sector for more than a century. The success story started in 1864, when the first tourist board in Switzerland was founded. Fourteen years later, St. Moritz became the first place in Switzerland with electric lights, while the first telephone in Graubünden was installed in the small village in 1886. In 1896, tourists visiting St. Moritz were surprised to see the first electric tram in the Alps. With the registration of the sun symbol in 1937 and the characteristic script of the name St. Moritz in 1986, the holiday resort became the first community to protect itself from imitation and to claim intellectual property rights. Since 1987, the entire logo, including the 'Top of the World' slogan, has been protected in more than fifty countries for up to fifteen product brackets. However, what is behind the trademark?

According to the head of the tourist board, St. Moritz is the 'last real epicurean and hedonistic paradise, where beautiful people of a certain standard from all over the world meet'. These tourists enjoy a symbiosis of nature and comfort, relishing the 'champagne climate' of St. Moritz. Some competitors might question why these cosmopolitan tourists feel drawn to St. Moritz. What distinguishes St. Moritz from other resorts that have not managed to achieve similar results? Obviously, it is more than the location or the climate, which St. Moritz shares with other holiday resorts. The difference lies in innovation management in terms of recognition, internalization and gradual conversion of trends. It also lies in the characteristics and management of the spirit of St. Moritz with its clear positioning, stability and strong leadership, all of which energize the community of independent actors, who together create a unique holiday environment.

ST. MORITZ – THE 'TOP OF THE WORLD'

Located 1,856 metres above sea level, St. Moritz is altitudinally closer to 'the top' than all of its famous competitors in Switzerland (Arosa: 1,815 metres; Zermatt: 1,620; Davos: 1,560; Gstaad: 1,050). In today's hedonistic world, the fact that the tourist board has managed to mobilize a large part of the community might appear to be a miracle to some outsiders. Even in St. Moritz, it is not possible to reach 100 per cent 'desirable' behaviour – the tourist board considers 60 per cent to be acceptable. Although 300 different and mostly independent teams engage in shaping St. Moritz's product programme, the village has managed to develop and sustain a spirit that combines the members of the community. For example, the organizing committees for new special events are normally financially supported by the tourist board for the first three years. Members of the tourist board are part of those teams, but they are not team leaders, and they normally try to hand over their responsibilities after the first three years. The long-term goal is for events to be autonomously financed and organized. The results are impressive:

★ First curling tournament on the Continent (1880)
★ First European ice-skating competition (1882)
★ First Olympic Games in Switzerland (1928 and 1948)
★ First modern winter sport: cresta (Skeleton) run (1885)
★ First golf tournament in the Alps on the Continent (1889)
★ First bob run (1890)
★ First horse race on snow (1906)
★ First horse race on a frozen lake (1907)
★ First ski school in Switzerland (1929)
★ First golf tournament on a snow-covered frozen lake (1979)
★ First polo tournament on a snow-covered frozen lake (1985)
★ First snowboard world championship on the Continent (1987)
★ First cricket tournament on a snow-covered frozen lake (1989)
★ First bob-run skating race (1991)
★ First windsurfing world cup for professionals in the Alps (1994)
★ First British classic car meeting (1994)
★ First polo world championships in the Alps (1995)
★ First inline skating marathon (1996)

This ambition of being 'Top of the World' leads the activities towards a common purpose based on clear positioning in the market, the stability of the key players in the community and strong leadership:

★ *Positioning*: the stirring slogan 'St. Moritz – Top of the World' is somewhat burdensome. Some St. Moritz residents and employees hate this slogan because it constantly goads them to outperform themselves and it serves as a benchmark for all activities. Distinct from the slogans of other holiday resorts, this slogan contains a strong imperative: to provide premium services to a very demanding international clientele. Slogans such as *Davos isch famos* (Davos is splendid) or *z'Sedrun wirsch brun* (In Sedrun, you will get a tan) do not have the same effect. The tourist board knew that it would be difficult to gain the approval of the entire community to introduce the slogan. It therefore decided to give the various actors no time to reflect on an alternative. The tourist board presented 'Top of the World' at a regular meeting and asked for other suggestions. As no one was prepared to offer any, they decided to accept their own proposal. It took more than ten years, but the slogan is now in the hearts and minds of most St. Moritz residents. Moreover, it is impossible to change the slogan because then St. Moritz would no longer be at 'the top'.

★ *Stability*: St. Moritz derives stability in the actions of its key players from its slogan. This expresses itself in the high number of regular guests – about two-thirds of all visitors. These guests meet each other year after year, which creates a family atmosphere. The tourist board supports customer retention by initiating clubs, annual events and special awards for repeated participation in the various events. Therefore, for example, a lot of British guests come back to the mountain resort. The tourist board is proud of this fact and sometimes describes St. Moritz as 'the last *functioning* British colony'. Along with the strong slogan and brand name comes the continuous cooperation with other brands, such as Rolex, Swissair, Cartier and Credit Swiss. The value of the 'St. Moritz' brand name is reflected in the fact that most partners use the name in their marketing campaigns – and St. Moritz gets this marketing for free. Consequently, the tourist board is very selective in its choice of partners, as those partners have to fit with the image of St. Moritz, and they must not offend existing customers and partners.

★ *Leadership*: hotel managers are sometimes described as 'pathological individuals', and it is often difficult to directly influence their behaviour. The same can be said of ski instructors, local authorities or shop owners. This makes the tasks of pushing the village in a common direction and invigorating actors' activities very difficult. The tourist board attempts to manage this task by cooperating with members of this network on an individual basis. When a new event is on the agenda, the tourist board tries to identify relevant junctions in the community network and works toward their involvement in the organizing committee. In that way, teams are self-organized and have a high likelihood of success. Another important leadership tool is the media. Whenever the tourist board has a valid customer complaint, it is published in the local press, where the tourist board has a column three times a week. Sometimes, the names of the offending persons are listed. The tourist board also uses the column to inform the community about planned activities. This ensures constant feedback. If the feedback does not come in time, the residents can only blame themselves for being tardy. In addition, television and radio are used to communicate with the mountain resort. The local radio station is especially effective. Whenever the tourist board has something important to say, it organizes an interview with the local radio station, which it uses to elaborate on current issues.

Firms can learn from how to stay 'On Top of the World' from St. Moritz. They can learn how trends are recognized, internalized and converted into competences and products by engaging many relatively independent actors without losing focus. The tourist board knows that because the world is constantly changing, the 'Top' is changing as well. Through the constant push for innovative solutions, experimentation, acceptance of failure and a strong cooperative network, new peaks are constantly created and then climbed.

A TYPICAL REORGANIZATION PATH: BACK TO CORE BUSINESS

In 2010, the CEO of France Telecom, Stéphane Richard, developed a five-year plan that included decommissioning the company's television business and returning to what was considered its primary business. In fact, executives around the world are beginning to understand the importance of focus in ensuring positive, stable performance over time. As in a typical restructuring process, superfluous activities or units must be sold, and the focus should shift to the core business. A company is more likely to be resilient when it does not extend itself beyond its core business but instead remains in businesses that serve basic customer needs. Companies that, for example, focus on food or pharma are genuinely more resilient:

> Socrates attended the agora of Athens, listening to the chatter in the square and observed the goods, material goods. To the disciples who asked him why, he replied: 'Why to discover all the things that I do not need'.
> (Cardinal Gianfranco Ravasi)

Under the leadership of former CEO Didier Lombard, France Telecom invested heavily in the acquisition of exclusive channels through the Orange brand for its pay-TV premium channels. The strategy aimed at increasing subscriptions to the Orange service and the dedicated platform. However, these operations did not have the desired benefits, and the company soon realized that the television industry is far removed from the telecommunications business. For this reason, Richard decided in 2012 to change course and invest in fibre-optic LTE networks, which were useful for developing the core business.

Similarly, Puma set a goal to decrease its product portfolio by 30 per cent by 2015. It chose to dedicate itself to focal products, such as shoes and sportswear.

Turnarounds were not new to Puma – in the early 1990s, after serious financial difficulties, Puma decided to focus on its core business. Meticulous outsourcing, the reorganization of activities in relation to autonomous profit centres, the re-engineering of key routines, the systematic reduction of costs, and a concentration on its football and running core businesses ensured that the company was able to establish a solid basis for further investments.

Kuzuo Hirai, CEO of Sony since 2012, recently stated that Sony was returning to its digital, games and mobile core, as 'this is the only way to be profitable and stable in the long run' (CNBC, 26 February 2013). [7] A few months earlier, Sony sold its chemical activities to a government-backed bank. Sony is now relying on an expected increase in annual smartphone sales from 33 million to 42 million units, and on higher revenues from video-game software. The return to profit promised by the CEO was only made possible by an acceleration of the disposal of accessory businesses; the sale of the headquarters in Manhattan, which were moved to 'Sony City' in Tokyo; the sale of a stake in M3 and the sale of the entire shareholding in DeNa (an electronics manufacturer). Other significant sacrifices were also made. For example, all of Sony's top forty managers waived their annual bonuses (equal to 30–40% of their salaries) in 2012. Masaru Kato, the CFO, did not hesitate to explain the reasons for the collective bonus waiver: the company was at the beginning of a path to sustainable profitability, but the start of the recovery required heavy sacrifices. In fact, for the first time in five years, the group closed the year in the black with an operating profit of JPY 230.1 billion (USD 2.45 billion; previous loss: JPY 67.3 billion) and a net profit of JPY 43 billion compared to the previous shocking loss of JPY 456.7 billion. In 2012, Sony had 5,500 fewer employees than it had the previous year owing to plant closures, redundancies and the disposal of assets (Il Sole 24 ORE, 5 June 2012).[8] The company's new path is marked by a focus on core businesses. In February 2014, Sony Corporation decided to sell its Vaio computer division to a Japanese investment fund because the business was deemed insufficiently profitable. The Vaio PC line was therefore assigned to the Japan Industrial Partners (JIP) fund, with Sony taking a minority shareholding in the fund through an equity stake of 5 per cent (*La Stampa*, 6 February 2014)[9].

In 2003, Cisco, the leader in business-information systems, bought Linksys, which was becoming a dominant actor in the household consumption network.

---

[7] See 'Sony CEO: Concentrating on core business' at: http://video.cnbc.com /gallery/?video=3000150469.

[8] See 'Sony perde il passo nell'innovazione' at: www.ilsole24ore.com/art/commenti-e -idee/2012-06-05/sony-perde-passo-innovazione-074324.shtml?uuid=AbcWXUnF&fromSearch.

[9] See 'Sony cede I PC Vaio' at: www.lastampa.it/2014/02/06/tecnologia/sony-cede-i-pc-vaio -h4cpbL8UxzTZOUDppnhREP/pagina.html.

As a result of the acquisition, Cisco found itself operating in two vastly different product segments with different sales models. In order not to lose sight of its product focus, Cisco decided to dispose of Linksys in 2012 and return its focus to its main business area (*Corporate Information Technologies*, 18 December 2012).[10]

Companies that are focused on specific niches are more likely to enjoy good financial results. Rollon, for example, is a leading manufacturer of linear motion guides. Its 2012 turnover totalled EUR 53.7 million, which represented an increase of 6 per cent compared to 2011 and an increase of 46 per cent compared to 2010. With 270 employees, the Milan-based company with subsidiaries in France, Germany and the United States is active in a niche market that is worth EUR 2.5 billion worldwide (La Repubblica 26 October 2015)[11].

An example of a small business is Elettrotec, a company with thirty employees that is managed according to its own vision of a pocket-sized multinational. Founded in 1977 by Pietro Cremaschi, the company originally sold hydraulic power packs and clutches for machine tools. After Cremaschi's death in 2001, his wife, Adriana Sartor, took over the reins. Today, Elettrotec designs and develops fluid-control instruments, a niche that produces an impressive turnover and has not felt the crisis (*Elettrottec*, 7 December 2013).[12]

WHY PORTFOLIO MATRICES OFTEN LEAD TO POOR BUSINESS DECISIONS

How can firms construct a meaningful portfolio of businesses? Firms frequently use portfolio matrices to make resource-allocation decisions at the corporate level. The most prominent of those portfolio matrices is the Boston Consulting Group (BCG) matrix. BCG claims that the four different business categories in the matrix's squares have different tendencies to generate or consume cash, and that they therefore need to be treated accordingly:

★ 'Question mark' businesses (high growth and relatively low market share) have high cash needs. Firms involved in such businesses should do whatever is necessary to increase market share or divest quickly.

---

[10] See 'Back to the future: CISCO announces its intentions to refocus on core business products' at: www.corp-infotech.com/2012/12/back-to-the-future-cisco-announces-its-intentions-to-refocus-on-core-business-products/.

[11] See 'Il mondo scorrevole vale 3 milardi' at: www.repubblica.it/economia/affari-e-finanza/2015/10/26/news/il_mondo_scorrevole_vale_3_miliardi_e_un_brand_tricolore_sfida_il_mercato-125967221/.

[12] See 'Verso nuovi confine' at: www.elettrotec.it/elettrotec/upload/allegati/Adriana_Sartor_tecne-low.pdf.

★ 'Star' businesses (high growth and relatively high market share) are frequently roughly in balance in terms of net cash flow and may sometimes need more cash than what is generated by their own business. The main focus of star businesses is to protect market share. To do so, they must get a bigger portion of market growth than their competitors. Star businesses will ultimately turn into cash cows, assuming that markets cannot grow forever. Alternatively, they can become dogs if they fail to protect their market share.

★ 'Cash cow' businesses (low growth and relatively high market share) are characterized by high profit and good cash generation. The cash that remains after covering the costs of running the business and protecting market share in a mature market should be redistributed to other businesses.

★ 'Dog' businesses (low growth and relatively low market share) often generate poor profits, and cash needs are frequently higher than the cash that is generated. To improve overall performance, firms should minimize the proportion of their assets that remains in this category by focusing on a specialized segment, by cutting costs, or by maximizing cash flow through divestments or liquidations.

The BCG matrix and other portfolio-planning tools have long occupied a fundamental position in corporate planning departments and in business school courses. In fact, the BCG growth share matrix – and its close relatives (most prominently the GE/McKinsey matrix) – is one of the best known and most persistent tools in strategic management. At the height of its success between 1972 and 1982, the BCG matrix was used by around 45 per cent of the Fortune 500 companies. In 1975, the prominent strategy scholar, Peter Lorange, asserted that the growth share matrix had become the common method of corporate planning.

The apparent simplicity of reducing a complex-decision problem to a two-dimensional matrix had intuitive appeal. The central assumption was based on academic research (i.e. the PIMS study), and managers located in corporate headquarters were able to show the value added by their businesses. The proliferation of portfolio planning as a resource-allocation tool was accelerated by BCG and its competitors, including McKinsey and Arthur D. Little, which developed similar matrixes together with their clients.

The BCG matrix explicitly recognizes that a diversified company encompasses a portfolio of businesses, each of which makes a distinct contribution to overall corporate performance and should be managed accordingly. Portfolio planning has its roots in the late 1960s when firms began becoming larger and more diversified. Corporate headquarters were created with the aim of adding value to their collection of businesses by allocating funds, creating synergies or directly influencing their activities. A central concern of corporate managers was to allocate funds in a strategic way and, thereby, ensure that the company balanced the cash needs of its business units. Alternative resource-allocation methods, such as basing investment decisions on track records or complex predictions of discounted project cash flows, did not seem to entirely satisfy corporate managers. In contrast, the BCG matrix helps to allocate limited resources based on a single graph. As such, it serves as a simplifier that links a single market dimension (i.e. market growth) to a single company dimension (i.e. relative market share).

However, the BCG matrix suffers from a number of flaws and its application is rather problematic. Assume for a moment that you are running a business unit that has been classified as a 'cash cow' because of its limited market attractiveness (in terms of market growth, market size and intensity of competition) and its dominant market position (in terms of relative market share, technological strength and brand name). In line with the portfolio logic, your CEO has decided to 'milk' your business and will not let you make substantial investments. What arguments can you use to convince your CEO that not investing in your business is a mistake?

The pitfalls of portfolio matrices include the following:

1   *Importance of market share*: a relationship between market share and profitability is not always present. The portfolio-matrix logic usually places too much emphasis on cost leadership and not enough focus on differentiation as a source of competitive advantage. For example, what is the role of the market shares held by Hermès, Ferrari or the full-time MBA programme at SDA Bocconi?

2   *Measurement problems*: relative market share depends on how the market is defined and that definition is rather subjective. A narrow definition of the reference market can turn a question mark into a star. Both axes – relative market share and market growth – depend on managers' subjective interpretations of what the relevant market is. Broad versus narrow definitions of markets reflect different views on the long-term development of a business. In many markets, it is difficult to gather data about total market size, growth rates and market shares, not to mention the challenges associated with the measurement and forecasting of product lifecycles. The effects of relaunches, technological innovation and facelifts on product lifecycles are highly uncertain and further

complicate growth predictions. These measurement problems may lead to different recommendations for the same situation.

3 *Assumptions about the product lifecycle*: the chronological sequence of questions marks (start-up) becoming stars (growth), then cash-cows (maturity) and eventually dogs (turnaround or decline/sale) has not proven applicable to all businesses. Consider, for example, Coca-Cola or Aspirin, which have been stars for a very long time. However, even poor dogs (which were initially labelled 'pets') often compete against lazy cash cows and dying dogs, and therefore provide stable cash flows – sometimes more cash than the question-mark businesses burn. Hence, the generic suggestion to 'milk' or 'divest' might be misleading.

4 *Oversimplistic*: the BCG model's use of only two dimensions (i.e. growth and share) to assess competitive positioning has been partly offset by including other elements to assess market attractiveness and relative strengths. However, it remains a relatively simple representation of realty. While this partly explains the attractiveness of the model for managers, we need to be aware of the pitfall of blindly following the model's indications.

5 *Hard to implement generic strategies*: when the corporate level has allocated a certain amount of money to a single business unit, the problem of allocating the money to individual projects remains. Another major implementation problem is the difficulty of unequivocally operationalizing strategic guidelines, such as 'milk for cash', 'harvest' or 'selectively invest'. Although intuitively appealing, those normative strategies need to be contextualized and refined. The BCG logic implies that firms have the ability to shift resources from one business to another. In capital-intensive and politically sensitive businesses, it might be costly to liquidate or divest a dog business. Barriers to exit due to legal or political constraints may complicate the implementation of the BCG guidelines. Even though there is usually a private equity fund or an emerging-market MNE willing to buy a dog business if the price is right, many firms are not good at divesting businesses. These firms could learn from Richard Branson, who has done a brilliant job of exiting dog businesses by floating them or selling them (in whole or part) to other companies. Consider, for example, the airlines Virgin Atlantic, Virgin America and Virgin Australia; the telecom businesses Virgin Mobile and Virgin Media; and the health-club chain Virgin Active.

6 *Synergies are not considered*: portfolio matrices tend to focus on balancing cash flows rather than on other interdependencies. For example, not investing in cash cows or didivesting dogs may imply that the star

businesses lose access to resources and capabilities that are essential for their development. This phenomenon has been labelled the 'phantom limb' effect of business divestment. In other words, missing links between business units hurt company performance, similar to the phantom pain some patients feel for years after they have lost a limb. Some matrices remedy this problem by including 'synergies' in the list of factors they consider when assessing relative strengths. However, the basic problem remains: we are using a portfolio approach for companies that are simply not portfolios of (independent) businesses.

7   *Backward looking*: the positioning of all businesses according to their relative market share and their market growth results in a one-spot representation of the business portfolio. The goal of management should be to have a balanced portfolio that can ensure optimization of the cash streams and, thereby, the overall performance of the company. Hence, the sustainable growth rate of a company is a function of its portfolio of cash-generating businesses and its cash-using businesses. The experience-curve effect explains why high market share businesses generate more cash than they can meaningfully redeploy and therefore create opportunities for new businesses in growing markets. However, data on recent market growth is not a good indicator of likely market growth in the future. For example, for producers of luxury goods, the 'star' markets of China and Brazil do not look very attractive in 2015.

8   *Perception biases*: simple labels have a huge influence on how people assess objects (e.g. if someone has been labelled 'a genius', everything that person does tends to confirm that perception in our minds). The BCG matrix attaches very broad and imprecise labels to business units that continually influence how those units are perceived within the organization. The labels also influence how top management filters information about those units. Along these lines, you can undertake a simple test: take an investment opportunity and see whether it is assessed differently based on whether it is coming from a star or a dog business simply because everything associated with the 'dog' label is perceived more negatively in the minds of managers.

We agree that a well-constructed portfolio matrix can support resource-allocation decisions. However, as with most management tools, it should only serve as a basis for discussion, and it should be complemented with other approaches, such as the valuation of concrete investment proposals (DCF method) or the evaluation of the applicant's past success. Therefore, the next time your management team tries to 'milk' your cash-cow business or 'divest' your dog business, use some of the arguments listed above to get attention for your alternative investment proposal.

Product focus increases organizational resilience. In fact, it allows you to be absolutely recognizable in the minds of consumers and invokes concepts of type authenticity (Carroll and Wheaton, 2009). For an overview of the concept of authenticity, we refer the reader to Chapter 4. Here, we highlight that consumers have more trust in something that is well defined – doing many things does not matter. The important thing is to take on a few activities but do them well.

DOES YOUR FIRM HAVE THE RIGHT PRODUCT FOCUS?

Our research suggests that high product focus increases resilience and, in turn, produces sustained superior performance. To assess the extent to which a firm is product focused, use this quick test. The various factors can be evaluated on a scale from 1 to 5 (where 1 = strongly disagree and 5 = completely agree) and relate to resilience-related actions that can be introduced in the company. You are free to modify the tool and integrate the short questionnaire with other items or indicators that are already used to measure performance in various areas of the firm.

Table 5.1 **Assess your firm's product focus**

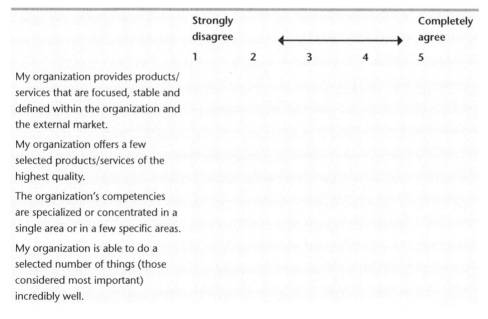

	Strongly disagree				Completely agree
	1	2	3	4	5
My organization provides products/ services that are focused, stable and defined within the organization and the external market.					
My organization offers a few selected products/services of the highest quality.					
The organization's competencies are specialized or concentrated in a single area or in a few specific areas.					
My organization is able to do a selected number of things (those considered most important) incredibly well.					

Table 5.1 (cont.)

	Strongly disagree				Completely agree
	1	2	3	4	5
Product focus score (the average of the four answers)					
Reference grid	1–2: Low resilience. You are not prepared for external shocks and need to invest in a resilience program.				
	3: Average resilience. Identify blind resilience spots and work on them.				
	4–5: High resilience. Stay the course. Make sure you stay alert.				

Source: Adapted from Conant, Mokwa and Varadarajan (2006).

CHAPTER 6

Geographical Focus

International diversification can be defined as expanding beyond national borders in different regions and markets (Hitt, Hoskisson and Kim, 1997). Geographical expansion entails both costs (Tallman and Li, 1996) and benefits (Geringer, Beamish and da Costa, 1989), and the trade-off can lead to different performance evaluations (Hitt, Hoskisson and Kim, 1997; Sullivan, 1994). Similar to our discussion of product diversification, the extant literature on the relationship between international expansion and performance does not offer clear results. When represented graphically with the level of international diversification on the x-axis and the performance achieved on the y-axis, the relation has been shown as linear or as having a more complex curve, such as a U shape (Lu and Beamish, 2001), an inverted-U shape (Hitt, Hoskisson and Kim, 1997) or an S-curve shape (Lu and Beamish, 2001).

In terms of high- and low-VOLARE companies, the more resilient companies are those that are cautious in their internationalization process. This essentially means two things: (1) investing in and maintaining a strong core (home) market as a source of strength, and (2) selectively investing in coherent geographical areas or those that are strategic for the business with the aim of achieving a strong position in those markets.

For example, among the resilient companies in the home-appliance sector, Miele and BSH have a strong European footprint. Miele generates 80 per cent of its revenue in Europe, while the corresponding figure for BSH is more than 75 per cent. Whirlpool is internationalized with a strong focus on the North American market (over 50% of revenue). The Swedish bank SEB has invested most of its resources in emerging markets. In the telecommunications sector, Swisscom is active in Switzerland and Italy, while China Mobile has a strong locational advantage because it operates only in China and Hong Kong. In banking, Scotiabank claims to be the most internationalized bank in Canada, but the majority of its revenue comes from the Canadian market. Its internationalization policy focuses on a few selected markets in Asia and Latin

America. The Indian bank HDFC keeps a tight focus on the Indian market. In an interview with Anil Jaggia, who is CIO of HDFC Bank, we asked whether the company had deliberately decided to maintain a presence in only the Indian market or if it was the company's intention to invest in new markets. Jaggia stated: 'We do not need to internationalize. We should not have to. What is wrong with having 30% growth in our own market? Honestly, we are fine where we are. We have small but widespread branches in our territory, and it works.' In addition, the previously discussed Italian master-craft enterprises are focused on markets that are not physically or culturally distant from their home markets.

Some of the companies interviewed (71%) stated that they had access to foreign markets through export activities, with 33 per cent of respondents reporting that they export more than 60 per cent of their turnover. Western Europe and the United States are the main foreign target markets, which reflects the need for a certain degree of focalization and cultural consistency in the choice of target markets. This conclusion assumes greater relevance for high-end companies, for which belonging to a specific local context is critical for maintaining competitive advantage.

We believe that international expansion increases the resilience of firms, at least to some extent. A study conducted by faculty from Bocconi University (Dallocchio M., Lussana F. and Vizzaccaro M, forthcoming article on a sample of Italian small and medium enterprises shows that Italian internationalized companies perform better in terms of return on equity (ROE) than non-internationalized enterprises. Based on data from 2004 to 2013, the research shows that firms generally experienced a decline in profitability in 2009 when the financial crisis plagued the real economy. However, the recovery of inter-nationalized companies was faster and more consistent than the recovery of non-internationalized companies, which still continue to show significant weaknesses. Notably, of the internationalized companies, those that perform best are those that are active in fewer countries. Moreover, those that per-form better have implemented their internationalization strategies in geo-graphical areas that are 'culturally' close – Western Europe (43% of cases) and North America (23% of cases). The worst performers are more active in Eastern Europe (17%) and Asia (23%).

As with product-related strategies, over-diversification may occur quickly when selecting geographical markets in which to operate. A focus on a few markets seems to be beneficial. Specifically, in order to ensure greater resil-ience and, therefore, a high level of VOLARE, at least four general principles apply when managing internationalization:

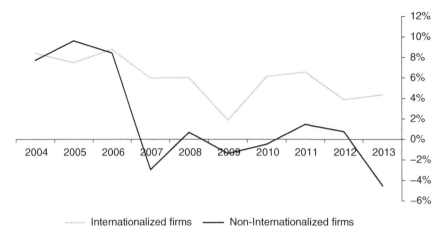

Figure 6.1 Performance of Italian internationalized SMEs relative to non-internationalized Italian firms

Source: authors' own based on AIDA data

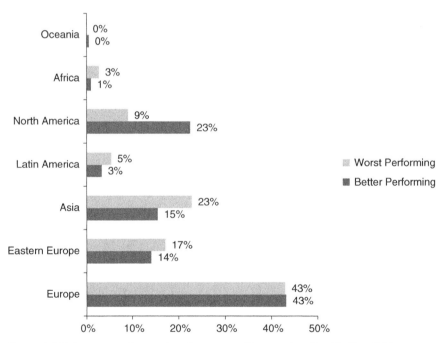

Figure 6.2 Reference markets and performance of internationalized Italian SMEs

Source: authors' own based on AIDA data

SIZE ALONE DOES NOT COUNT[1]

Companies often internationalize in order to grow in size and to exploit the economies of scale derived from such growth. However, a detailed analysis of the banking sector, for example, shows that the relationship between size and performance does not seem relevant. Among the top ten banks in terms of assets in 2008 were UBS, The Royal Bank of Scotland, Citigroup and Deutsche Bank. All have since suffered heavily from the effects of the crisis and have not yet fully recovered. In contrast, small and more focused banks, such as HDFC, Canadian Western Bank and Banco de Chile, were able to maintain good performance despite the volatility of the external environment. Figure 6.3 shows that no bank in excess of USD 700 billion has a high VOLARE.

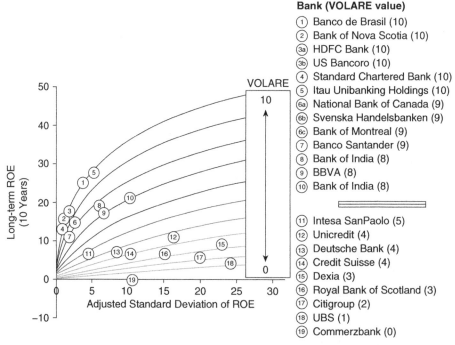

Figure 6.3 Banking sector VOLARE: best and worst performers[2]

Source: Markman and Venzin (2014)

[1] This section is based on Markman and Venzin, Resilience: Lessons from banks that have braved the economic crisis – and from those that have not, *International Business Review*, 2014, **23**, 1096–107, DOI: 10.1016.
[2] Markman and Venzin, op. cit.

Banco Santander is the largest bank with a high VOLARE (VOLARE 9). This bank operates in a difficult domestic market (Spain), and it is large and geographically diverse. Our interviews with managers and executives as well as our analysis of internal and external reports suggest that Banco Santander's performance is not due to its size per se, but rather to the fact that the bank adheres to the 'ownership, location and internationalization' paradigm (Dunning, 1988; Parada, Alemany and Planellas, 2009). First, the Spanish bank has developed strong organizational skills, prudent risk management, and a strict focus on retail and commercial banking. Second, it has developed and improved these competencies by relying on and dominating its home market. Finally, the bank began its international expansion by investing in culturally similar and geographically close markets. For example, it acquired the United Kingdom's Abbey National in 2004 and then transferred the competencies developed in the domestic market to that foreign subsidiary to ensure significant cost savings.

With the exception of Banco Santander (and a few others with even lower levels of VOLARE, e.g. Wells Fargo, HSBC and BNP Paribas, all with VOLARE 7), we can see from Figure 6.4 that the big banks (in terms of assets) bear a 'liability of size'. In other words, they underperform their smaller competitors in terms of financial results achieved in the long run and risk.

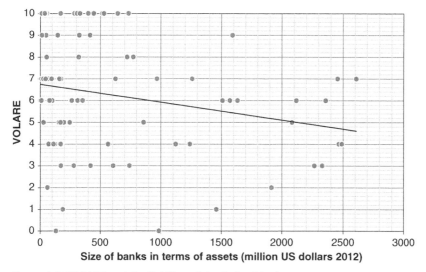

Figure 6.4 VOLARE and the liability of size in banking[3]
Source: Markman andVenzin (2014)

[3] Markman and Venzin, op. cit.

Being a very large company in conjunction with high-growth rates, especially double-digit growth, is difficult to manage in the long term and greatly increases complexity (Venzin, 2004). For example, consider two of the largest and oldest multinationals: Procter and Gamble (P&G), and Citigroup. In 2012, P&G, with annual revenue of USD 80 billion, turned 175 years old. Citigroup, with annual revenue of USD 71 billion, celebrated 200 years in business. P&G grows by 5 per cent each year, which does not seem to be an overly ambitious goal. Given its size, such growth implies that a single P&G subsidiary like ACE (a P&G detergent brand that is 65 years old) is comparable in size to the entirety of Hasbro, one of the largest toy producers in the world (and 90 years old). In the same way as an oil tanker must begin to slow down 60 kilometres from the coast in order to avoid a possible collision, large size can create rigidity and paralysis in management. Everything becomes more complex.

The liability of size is not limited to stalled growth. Size can also lead to vulnerabilities that were considered unlikely until the recent economic and financial crisis. In other words, modern portfolio theories, mergers and acquisitions, and studies of diversification all converge on the logic that companies need to diversify their assets in different markets in order to reduce risk. International business research shows that multinational companies use foreign markets to reduce risk and disperse shocks, which they cannot do in the single domestic market.

We are not claiming that small size implies immunity to shocks. Many small and medium-sized enterprises have been swept away by the crisis. However, we stress that being large is not enough to ensure good and stable performance over time. Llewellyn (2002) argues that long-term survival is more related to the ability to create focused and efficient strategies than to increasing size. A focus on becoming bigger that underestimates other elements, such as product integration, organizational synergies across countries and business ethics, can adversely affect performance (Carmeli and Markman, 2011). A balanced and sustainable approach to growth is, in this sense, the way to produce better results and a main strategic need for the vast majority of European companies, which are mostly (99%)[4] small or medium in size (as defined by the European Commission in 2006),[5] and for which greater sustainable size would mean

---

[4] MISE (Ministry of Economic Development) on Cambridge Econometrics, 2012.
[5] Micro companies: < 10 work units per year; ≤ EUR 2 million in annual revenue; ≤ EUR 2 million in annual total assets.

    Small companies: < 50 work units per year; ≤ EUR 10 million in annual revenue; ≤ EUR 10 million in annual total assets.

    Medium companies: < 250 work units per year; ≤ EUR 50 million in annual revenue; ≤ EUR 43 million in annual total assets.

easier access to credit, greater investment capacity, greater bargaining power and better management of internationalization strategies.

Internal processes, such as the cost structure, and a well-formulated business model with high levels of customer centricity and elements of strategy evaluation, as well as emotional factors can have a greater impact on resilience than size alone. For example, Prysmian, a leader in the cable industry, pays attention to competition from large competitors, but it fears the effects that small rivals may have on their businesses. Status as a leader in itself means nothing. Status as a leader in the market of reference counts – the intersection of product and geography determines long-term success. In fact, Fabio Romeo, head of corporate strategy at Prysmian, claims that 'the global cable market does not exist'. In other words, there is no value in being the leader of a market that has many unrelated sub-segments.

THE IMPORTANCE OF THE DOMESTIC MARKET

The home market has a substantial impact on the achievement of positive and stable performance over time. In solid countries, such as Germany, the United Kingdom, Switzerland and the United States, many companies have top-level VOLARE. However, these markets are also home to some companies that have major problems due to the crisis. Good performance can also be found in less-stable and less-developed markets, such as Brazil or India. If we return to the example of Banco Santander, one might wonder how it managed to achieve excellent performance while operating in a market experiencing such great difficulties. Banco Santander operates in seven additional markets outside Spain. It has a market share in each of these markets of at least 10 per cent. These countries are considered 'home bases', namely markets in which to replicate the domestic model and become as strong as in the original home market. This explains how the institution obtained more than 55 per cent of its profits from emerging but lucrative markets, such as Brazil, in 2012.

Similarly, Vodafone (VOLARE 0), a fixed and mobile-telephony multinational, has its headquarters in Newbury in the United Kingdom. It has interests in twenty-five countries. In sixteen of those countries, it operates under its own brand. However, it does not hold a leading position in any of these markets, including the home market. It is always challenged by other companies that hold market leadership. Only recently, under the leadership of Vittorio Colao, has Vodafone started to exit a few markets (including the United States) in order to fortify its market position in a few core markets.

These examples illustrate that firms with a focused international presence tend to be more resilient than firms with a highly dispersed geographical footprint. In our view, it is generally better to be among the top three players in terms of market share in ten geographical or product segments than among the top ten players in thirty segments.

CAUTIOUS MANAGEMENT OF PRODUCT AND MARKET COMPLEXITY

Markman and Venzin (2014) ran a quantitative test on the banking sector to investigate whether the complexity of the product or the market affects the ability to generate stable and positive performance in the long term. They segmented the sector into nine geographical areas (e.g. Western Europe; Eastern Europe; Middle East and Turkey; the former Soviet Union; greater China and Hong Kong; East Asia and Japan; North America; and the rest of the world) and then analysed whether the banks in their sample were present in those regions. In a third step, to measure product complexity, six product categories were identified: transaction banking, corporate finance (e.g. mergers and acquisitions), financial market, private banking and asset/wealth management, personal banking (e.g. retail banking), and corporate banking (e.g. business loans, financing, leasing). Finally, the authors counted the number of product categories offered by each bank in each geographical region.

By calculating various indices, such as the Herfindahl index to measure industry concentration, the authors could calculate the impact of various variables on performance. Contrary to expectations, no relationship was found between presence in different markets or region-product diversity and financial performance. However, a positive relationship was found between product complexity and performance. The resilient banks are those that offer diversified products and know-how with regard to interpreting each as a source of profit. In addition, banks with a VOLARE of 10 and a high level of product complexity are those that are more geographically focused.

We can once again return to the example of Banco Santander. As noted previously, its international expansion strategy focuses on markets where there is a large possibility of obtaining leadership. The Spanish bank creates small growth opportunities through minority shareholdings or through its consumer banking business. Thereafter, based on the initial evidence, it decides whether to increase its commitment or effect a change of direction. For instance, Banco Santander bought the German DC-Bank and slowly transformed it into one of the most successful local banks by introducing the VISA credit card. Numerous other innovations were planned and implemented, such as mobile banking, and loans for dentures or vacations. These ideas enabled Banco Santander to achieving more than USD 14 billion in credit volume. In contrast, when the bank realized that its strategic alliance with The Royal Bank of Scotland did not bring many advantages, it concluded the partnership and withdrew from the market.

Banco Santander's incremental approach and its strong awareness of the risks associated with internationalization have been greatly influenced by the values and priorities of the Botin family, which serves as an example of entre-preneurship and caution. The CEO, Emilio Botin, applies a simple growth strategy: the bank acquires only foreign institutions with restructuring poten-tial and a minimum market share of 10 per cent. The bank stays away from businesses that it does not understand (e.g. investment banking).

The Indian bank HDFC (VOLARE 10) is even more cautious. In fact, it aims for performance without volatility. Our interviews with first-line managers indicate that its leader, Aditya Puri, 'wants stability and few fluctuations in the results. He does not want to obtain 1 in one year and 0 the next year. To do this, only stable business resources should be selected and our CEO is very good at this. Similarly, another interviewee stated:

> Whatever we do – micro finance, credit cards and so forth – we do it in the best way. We have a 31 per cent market share in credit cards. A single bank. Hard to believe. Whatever we do, we do it at a top level. If you issue a credit card to a customer, it must be the absolute best credit card ever. Loans, micro loans, micro finance, everything. We want to be in the top position. We want to be the best.

WHEN REDUCING INTERNATIONAL EXPOSURE INCREASES RESILIENCE

To reduce market and product complexity, firms sometimes have to substan-tially reduce their international presence. This may sound counter-intuitive, but our results indicate that higher degrees of geographical diversification actually increase the volatility of performance results. Think about Citigroup, one of the largest financial services company in the world. Following the 2008 crisis, Citigroup was in danger of collapsing, and it had to considerably reduce its international presence and number of employees. As early as 2007, Citigroup had begun to remove 5 per cent of jobs in an extensive restructur-ing project aimed at cutting costs. In November 2008, the ongoing crisis hit

Citigroup hard. Despite federal aid, the company announced another 100,000 layoffs. In addition, Citigroup and the federal regulators negotiated a plan to stabilize the company. The plan foresaw substantial downsizing in terms of presence in different geographic markets. This case demonstrates that being large does not always guarantee positive performance in absolute terms. At times, a large size creates paralysis and management difficulties in the face of external shocks.

Given this discussion, companies may wish to follow some basic rules when making internationalization decisions. The first is to consider the central domestic market, which plays a crucial role in determining performance. The second is to be cautious in expansion strategies. Targeted areas should be coherent and should almost represent a second home market. Companies should be careful to avoid venturing too far into unknown or distant markets, or into risky businesses. Michael Bjergby, Financial Risk Manager at Novo Nordisk, claims that: 'Novo Nordisk is risk averse. The tendency is always to take calculated risks, or the least possible risk. The risk to our business is already very high. We cannot have high financial risks.' Hence, if the complexity in products or markets increases greatly, then the focus should be on those things that the firm does well without getting carried away by an unbridled desire to extend boundaries. Informed, calculated choices, as opposed to an ingenious search for scale, seem to be the best path towards resilience.

THE CHOICE OF COHERENT AREAS

In keeping with this cautious approach to managing internationalization, one path pursued by more resilient companies seems to be to identify and subsequently select coherent areas for foreign expansion. The division of the world into areas that have certain characteristics in common seems to be a successful strategy in times of crisis. Investing in an additional foreign country requires effort not only in terms of time and resources. At times, finding a way to replicate home-market sources of competitive advantage in a specific country is hazardous. Once a recipe has been found, it seems more appropriate to invest resources in penetrating that specific market than to move on to the next market. Expansion into similar countries allows for optimization of effort. In this way, the set of emerging markets, such as European nations, can be considered as a single reference area. Aggregation on the basis of similarity can simplify things, but we must also recognize the limits of oversimplification. For example, many firms have suffered from considering APAC or China as a homogeneous market segment. However, clustering geographies in order to simplify general market approaches and create synergies is essential.

Fabrizio Longo, managing director of Hyundai Italy, told us that his company establishes regions on the basis of a well-chosen set of criteria:

> For us, Europe is as a region in its own right. I think it is very smart to not allow yourself to be blinded by the lights of the "World Car". The policies are absolutely consistent when viewed from a height of 10,000 metres, but dangerous when viewed from a lower level in the territory. For us, there is the European area, the American area, the Russian area, and those areas closest and most similar to Korea, where we began our investments.

Market coherence can also be determined by consumer behaviour. Rakesh Kapoor, CEO of Reckitt Benckiser, a multinational active in household cleaning with such product lines as Napisan and Durex, said that:

> even for foreign markets, we have created an organisation that differs substantially from those of our competitors, dividing them up into three major areas: ENA (Europe and North America), LAPAC (Latin America, Asia Pacific) and RUMEA (Russia, Middle East, Africa). No other group has ever put Europe and America together because there is an ocean in between. Our organisation is not divided according to geographical boundaries but according to consumer behaviour: the preferences, the European way of life are increasingly similar to the American.
>
> (*Corriere della Sera*, 1 September 2013)[6]

DO YOUR FIRM HAVE THE RIGHT GEOGRAPHICAL FOCUS?

Our research suggests that geographical focus increases resilience and, in turn, produces sustained superior performance. To assess whether a firm has the right geographical focus, use this quick test. The various factors can be evaluated on a scale from 1 to 5 (where 1 = strongly disagree and 5 = completely agree) and relate to resilience-related actions that can be introduced in the company. Of course, you are free to modify the tool and integrate the short questionnaire with other items or indicators that are already used to measure performance in various areas of the firm.

---

[6] See 'La rivoluzione geografica di Benckiser' at: www.pressreader.com/italy/corriere-della-sera/20130901/282402692049563.

Table 6.1 Assess your firm's geographical focus

	Strongly disagree				Completely agree
	1	2	3	4	5
My organization develops profound knowledge of the markets in which it operates, and adopts new services or selects new markets only after careful analysis of their potential.					
My organization carefully analyses costs and revenues with the goal of keeping costs under control and entering new markets on a selective basis.					
My organization prefers to be present in a few foreign markets with a high local market share instead of serving a larger number of foreign markets with lower market shares.					
The markets in which my organization operates can be aggregated into macro areas of converging and coherent interests.					
Market focus score (the average of the four answers)					
Reference grid	1–2: Low resilience. You are not prepared for external shocks and need to invest in a resilience programme.				
	3: Average resilience. Identify blind resilience spots and work on them.				
	4–5: High resilience. Stay the course. Make sure you stay alert.				

Source: Adapted from Conant, Mokwa and Varadarajan (2006).

CHAPTER 7

Long-term Orientation and Strategic Decision Making

Resilient firms are able to identify threats early, quickly decide how to react and swiftly implement those decisions. In volatile markets, the ability to make sound strategic decisions is the main source of competitive advantage. However, many firms struggle. One of the main problems in decision making lies in the lack of a long-term orientation. Many management teams reason mostly from a 'one day to the next' perspective and are always focused on immediate results. As such, they fail to consider what may happen in the future. The difficulty in considering the long term is that doing so often means going beyond one's own permanence in the position or even in the company.

In family businesses, where short-term pressure is generally less pronounced, the idea of a successor is not necessarily contemplated. However, there is a natural tendency for the retiring entrepreneur to leave the business in a state that is as good as possible. The passing of the baton between two generations is one of the most critical moments in the life of a family business – only about 15 per cent of family businesses survive to the third generation. The highly central role played by the entrepreneur makes his or her replacement difficult. In addition, the strong emotional involvement determined by family relationships often leads to decisions that are unable to balance the business logic and family values. Nevertheless, this problem is often overlooked by entrepreneurs, who tend to evade it or only partially deal with it. In a 2005 survey of 600 Italian companies, nearly 40 per cent of leaders indicated that they would work as long as possible and only 8 per cent had set a retirement age (Mezzadri, 2005).

In large companies, on the other hand, the length of job rotations is increasingly short, such that the working reality changes every few years. Newly appointed CEOs often go through four phases:

★ *Phase 1*: newly appointed CEOs take a few months to study the situation. Within the first few months, they declare that the situation is worse than they thought and issue a profit warning (for internally promoted CEOs, this process can be faster, as seen in Shell in 2013).

★ *Phase 2*: in the second year, CEOs start to implement strategic actions, making it clear that they need more time to produce positive results.

★ *Phase 3:* in the third year, CEOs focus on optimizing short-term profit, cutting strategic R & D and marketing investments, and increasing revenue through involvement in riskier projects.

★ *Phase 4*: in the fourth year, CEOs leave the company.

Our research suggests that worrying about the results of successors – even if this implies accepting lower profits now and taking the blame for that disappointment – increases the likelihood that a company will be resilient. A long-term orientation implies devoting time and effort to 'strategic' projects.

SETTING PRIORITIES

At the basis of strategic decision making lies a desire to build a better future for the coming decades. Think about the great architectural works that have survived centuries, from the pyramids to monuments and imposing cathedrals built hundreds of years ago. To build a church like the Cathedral of Milan required a certain amount of interest in creating value for future generations. The Cathedral was started in 1395. However, due to the difficulty of the case and the necessary investments, it was not completed until 1500. Today, there no longer seems to be the same desire to invest in projects with long-term horizons. Even institutional investors seem to invest in short-term projects. What should the investment horizon of a pension fund be? Certainly not less than one year.

Decision makers in resilient companies have a long-term perspective that goes beyond their tenures with the company, and beyond concerns for individual products or short-term goals. At the opening ceremony for the 2013–2014 academic year at Bocconi University, Vittorio Colao, CEO of Vodafone, said: 'My biggest challenge is to ensure that our decision makers have a long-term perspective.'

Think about the strategic plan promoted by the founder of Facebook, Mark Zuckerberg, whose goal is to make Internet access available to the poorest by pushing the reach of mobile connectivity. The plan is to reach five billion people who are currently excluded from the Web. The project is called 'Internet.org' and involves major players in the sector – from phone companies to microchip manufacturers to network specialists. The project intends to act on three main elements: to reduce the cost of smartphones, to increase the efficiency of data transmission and to develop new business models that enable companies to offer Internet access at a lower cost in countries involved in the project. As pointed out by the Facebook founder, the goal is to reduce the cost of mobile Internet access by 99 per cent and, thereby, extend the number of Internet users without excessive investments in networks (La Repubblica, 5 May 2015).[1] The project requires a focus on the long term and a vision that goes beyond the company's current activities.

Likewise, Richard Branson, founder of Virgin, is famous for his long-term view and visionary projects. The company Virgin Galactic, which he co-owns, should send the first space tourists into orbit soon if the tests allow. The company's experimental shuttle (SpaceShipTwo) passed a second important test by beating the previous height record and going beyond the 300-kilometre threshold. The shuttle will travel at supersonic speeds and will be able to accommodate six passengers at a time. It will float in the absence of gravity for about six minutes, while passengers look down at Earth. The ticket cost is estimated at USD 250,000 per person.[2]

The starting point for creating a long-term orientation is to focus management attention on important issues that are not urgent. Firms can use the Eisenhower matrix (Figure 7.1) to do so. The matrix helps the firm order its strategic issues according to the criteria of importance and urgency, as popularized by Steven Covey in his book *The Seven Habits of Highly Effective People* (Covey, 1989). Figure 7.1 shows the four types of situations that tend to be created in a company.

It is natural to focus on highly urgent matters, even if they are not important. Think about your recent strategy meetings. Many of them probably started with the good intention of understanding what the company should do in five to ten years but ended with a discussion of specific operational issues. Resilient firms have developed the capability to deal with important issues before they become urgent. Crises can be averted if major challenges are identified in time or, rather, if firms exercise their forecast abilities. Returning to the metaphor of a boxer, it is important to forecast the next punch and try to avoid it.

For example, when the dominant thought is that a single product innovation will ensure success over time, the orientation is short term. This is demonstrated by the many cases of prominent companies that have failed to look beyond their own technologies. Polaroid, for example, launched an

---

[1] See 'Nessun monopolio: Facebook apre Internet.org a sviluppatori esterni' at: www.repubblica .it/tecnologia/social-network/2015/05/05/news/facebook_internet-113593225/.
[2] *The Huffington Post*, 11 October 2013. See 'Viaggi nello spazio. Richard Branson manda in orbita i primi turisti nel 2014. Già 769 prenotazioni. Intervista al direttore della Onirikos' at: www.huffingtonpost.it/2013/10/11/viaggi-spaziali-branson_n_4083419.html.

The Eisenhower Matrix

DO FIRST	LESS URGENT
Important – Urgent Subject to confirming the importance and the urgency of these tasks, do these tasks now. Priorities according to their relative urgency.	**Important – Not Urgent** Critical to success: planning, strategic thinking, deciding direction and aims, etc. Plan time-slots and personal space for these tasks.
DELEGATE	DON'T DO
Not Important – Urgent Scrutinize and probe demands. Help orginators to re-assess. Wherever possible reject and avoid these tasks sensitively and immediately	**Not Important – Not Urgent** Habitual 'comforters' not true tasks. Non-productive, de-motivational. Minimize or cease altogether. Plan to avoid them.

Figure 7.1 The eisenhower matrix
Source: adapted from Stephen Covey (1989)

instant camera and achieved immediate global success. In time, however, it was unable to follow the changes in the industry or to adapt to digital technologies. As D'Aveni and Gunther argued in 1994, 'the world continues to move forward into hypercompetition ... we can stand still and allow this wave of constant change to wash over us ... Or we can actively embrace the environment and take advantage of its opportunities ... In a dynamic world only the dynamic survive'. According to the *Innovator's Dilemma* (Christensen, 1997), more successful firms in a given technological context find it structurally difficult to perceive the threat posed by new and disruptive technologies. Even if they were to perceive it, the rigidity of the decision-making process could prevent management from changing the strategy in time. A resilient company is able to disinvest in time and push for a new product to replace the old one.

WHERE DOES LONG-TERM ORIENTATION COME FROM?

A propensity to focus on the long term may derive from the personal inclinations of decision makers, as evidenced by the famous 'marshmallow' experiment at Stanford University. The study focused on deferred gratification and was conducted in 1972 by psychologist Walter Mischel. It is considered one of the most successful experiments on behaviour in the scientific field. Children were given a marshmallow (or similar snack) on a plate with the instruction: 'If you can wait to eat the marshmallow until I am back, you will get another one.' The scientists analysed the time that elapsed before each child gave in to the temptation to eat the marshmallow.

The purpose of the study was to investigate the control that children exercise when faced with an option for delayed gratification, namely the ability to wait to obtain what one wants. The initial experiment took place in a nursery school located at Stanford University, and involved four- to six-year-old children who were taken to an empty room where a snack of their choice (e.g. an Oreo cookie, a marshmallow or a pretzel) was placed on a table or a chair. The children were told that they could eat the snack. However, if they could wait fifteen minutes without giving in to temptation, they would be rewarded with a second snack. Mischel observed that some covered their eyes with their hands, turned away from the table so they would not see the snack, drummed their fingers, kicked the table, sang songs, counted numbers, twirled their hair and adopted all sorts of tactics to distract themselves. Some even licked, smelled or stroked the marshmallow. Of the more than 600 children who participated in the experiment, one-third were able to delay gratification long enough to obtain the second snack.

In subsequent years, Mischel monitored most of the six hundred children in his original experiment as they became adolescents and then adults using questionnaires measuring various aspects of their character and school career. A longitudinal study, carried out fourteen years later (at which time the children were almost of age) showed that those who had been able to exert cognitive control on their immediate impulses had the best scholastic results. More specifically, a positive correlation was found between the minutes they waited before eating the snack and their SAT scores (a test for college admission). The greediest (those who had immediately succumbed to temptation) were more likely to develop behavioural problems and low self-esteem. Moreover, they were more often viewed by others as stubborn, frustrated and envious. On average, their SAT scores were 210 points lower than those of their non-marshmallow-eating peers. The study showed that the ability to delay gratifications affected individual performance on many levels. However, an important question remained: is self-control an individual characteristic or can it be learned?

To answer this question required recruiting the children originally involved in the experiment at age forty and subjecting them to a new experiment. The results appeared in the article 'Behavioural and neural correlates of delay of gratification 40 years later' (Casey et al., 2011). The authors devised a new task that was similar to the original but age-appropriate. In this case, the individuals were placed in front of a screen and asked to press a button when the face of a man or woman appeared. After a few minutes, they were asked to only press the button when a smiling or sad face appeared. Then they were asked not to press the button when they saw a smiling face. This was the new marshmallow condition – reflection and cognitive control were required to resist the urge to press the button at the sight of something attractive, specifically a smile. The results showed that those who had pounced on the snacks when they were young were those who made more errors as adults. This suggests that the ability to control impulses is an individual characteristic that is relatively stable over time.

Similarly, George Loewenstein, a professor at Carnegie Mellon, carried out an experiment entitled 'celebrity kiss'. Students were promised a passionate kiss from a famous Hollywood actress/actor. The experiment asked how much they were willing to pay for that kiss if they had to wait for it for a specified period of time. They could decide to pay to receive the kiss in the next three hours, in twenty-four hours, in three days, in a year or in ten years. The results showed that the highest amount of money was offered to wait for three days (Figure 7.2).

This discussion suggests that the anticipation of what will be makes people happy if the wait is not too long. The idea of waiting for a limited time to receive a kiss from a Hollywood actress/actor was more appealing than receiving it immediately. However, it becomes difficult to wait longer than a certain period of time. The demand curve declines over time. What, then, can be done to help individuals and organizations develop a long-term orientation?

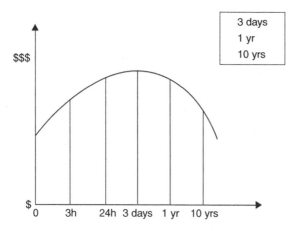

Figure 7.2 'Celebrity kiss' experiment results
Source: adapted from Loewenstein (2009)

Firms (or individuals) that are able to depict a clear picture of where they want to be in five to ten years have a better chance of developing strategies to get there. The opposite is also true. To motivate obese children to diet, scientists have shown them pictures of how they will look as adults. Management teams are shown 'worst-case scenarios' to get their attention for important issues. Too often, the fast-changing environment is used as an excuse for not planning and for not investing in organizational flexibility as a substitute for strategy. We agree that it is sometimes difficult to adopt a long-term orientation when looking at what is happening in the market or in the sector of reference (market-based view). The external environment is changing too fast to allow for a vision that goes beyond the short-term horizon, which is useful in addressing urgent and sudden changes of direction. However, firms can facilitate the creation of a long-term vision by adopting a perspective that complements the market-based view and links products and services to internal company resources and capabilities. This 'resource-based view' is often a better source of orientation because a firm's processes or resources change slower than customer preferences or other market conditions.

ORGANIZING FOR THE LONG- TERM

Firms need to invest time in thinking about the future. Unfortunately, it seems that creating a picture of where the company should be in five to ten years is not easy: 'The future is like heaven, everyone exalts it, but no one wants to go there now' (James Baldwin)[3]. The suggested formulae for looking at the long-term are manifold, but almost all involve a certain openness to change. Some companies are able to be 'farsighted'. This is the case for Scott Malkin, the son of a US real-estate baron, who owns a sizeable chunk of real estate in New York and reinvented the family business. Spurred by the first real-estate crisis in the United States, he transformed his company from classic real estate to ultra-luxury outlet real estate. One of the most famous in Italy is the Fidenza Village, which is located between Milan and Bologna. In 2012, the Chic Outlet Village business generated EUR 1.7 billion in sales from the nine Italian outlets. The idea was then to internationalize and turn to China. Thus, a high-end shopping mall near Shanghai, was born (Luxos, 26 march 2014)[4].

---

[3] James Arthur Baldwin (2 August 1924–1 December 1987) was an African American novelist, essayist, playwright, poet and social critic.

[4] See 'Value retail to open luxury shopping complex in China' at: www.luxos.com/news /fashion/4982-value-retail-opens-its-first-village-in-china-in-may.

In some cases, the issue is about having the courage to go against the grain. Raoul Ascari, COO of Italy's SACE, which operates in financial and insurance services, says:

> We need to form an 'opposite' mentality. Unfortunately, we tend to standardize thought. The best thing is to train people to be sceptical, not to take things as absolute truths. In recent years, we have heard many things that then turned out to be wrong. Knowledge has a very high rate of obsolescence. You know that spinach is good because it contains iron? Well, that is not true. The German chemist who studied the composition of spinach had misplaced a comma and a very high content of iron ensued (Arbesman, 2012). The children of a generation suffered eating spinach. So you think you know something but, in reality, you do not really know. What do we need in this world? The ability to use our heads.

Farsightedness sometimes means changing the target audience. An example is Huawei. The CEO of the Chinese colossus, Richard Yu, declared he no longer wanted to produce low-cost handsets, even for telecom operators. Instead, he claimed, his company was ready to directly confront Samsung and Apple, and to ensure medium-high quality standards. The strategy, common among internationalizing Chinese and Korean companies, is to appear on the market with basic products that follow the leader and then subsequently position the company to conquer the high-end range. It takes some foresight and probably a transition from one CEO to another to implement a strategy consisting of several moves. As such, a long-term orientation seems to be more widespread in Asian cultures.

In Haier,

> the first strategy for going abroad was to fit into a niche market. This was the case for mini fridges and wine cellars proposed to the US market. In 2004, Haier captured 30 per cent of the market for small refrigerators in the US, 50 per cent of the US market in wine cellars and one-tenth of the market for air conditioners in Europe. Since then, the international policy has become increasingly aggressive. In every market, Haier has attempted to identify and meet local demands by gradually increasing the quality of the product.
>
> (interview with Enrico Ligabue, managing director,
> Haier Italy and Greece)

To manage the long term, firms have to develop ambidexterity – the capability to survive the present by exploiting existing resources and competences, and to prepare for future success by exploring new options. Splitting capabilities through time (i.e. going through phases of 'survival' or exploitation followed by periods of focusing on 'advancement' or exploration) or space (i.e. creating specific units that take care of 'advancement' tasks), but providing for both allows an organization to have both a short-term orientation and long-term vision. One function manages *execution* and the other handles *transformation*. In Google, the ambidexterity practice has become consolidated. Engineers have one day a week to work on a project of their choice. Services such as Gmail, Google Earth, Orkut and AdSense were born out of this freedom of choice. Managers are also required to allocate a portion of their time to innovation. More specifically, they must dedicate 70 per cent of their time to the core business, 20 per cent to different but related projects, and 10 per cent to entirely new projects and business. The company has recently created a new position – the 'Director of Other' – to help manage the latter 10 per cent.

Another way for companies to facilitate long-term thinking and acting is through incentives. A sophisticated system of incentives linked to long-term strategic goals increases organizational resilience. Most of an organization's internal and external activities can be explained in terms of its system of incentives (Clark and Wilson, 1961). The incentive system should be aligned with the type of company (e.g. utilitarian companies, solidaritarian companies and those focused on objectives). This alignment becomes even more important in times of crisis. In the face of considerable external shocks, companies cannot simply focus on the achievement of short-term profit but must formulate their strategies to achieve long-term goals – and they must measure and motivate results. Our study indicates that resilient firms have incentives that are relatively sophisticated. They typically have:

★   An incentive system linked not only to financial performance but also to
    the wider strategic objectives.
★   A system that is formed of different parts, including a fixed part, and
    a variable or share-based part that provides bonuses when things go
    particularly well.

AstraZeneca, for example, links the remuneration of its executives to a well-articulated balanced scorecard. GSK awards bonuses to R & D employees based on their productivity. Novo Nordisk compensates its executives using a fixed rate reduced from 40–60 per cent to 35–55 per cent to which are added cash-and share-based incentives. The share-based part is calibrated on the basis of ambitious targets for company reputation, employee training and relations with the external environment. In Hyundai, says Fabrizio Longo,

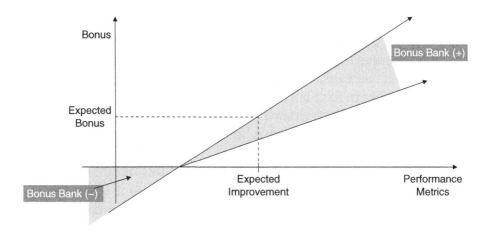

Figure 7.3 Bonus bank and expected performance
Source: adapted from the 2009 Stern Stewart Report[5]

'incentives were once only of a quantitative nature. Now a quality element has been added based on the long term. For example, the commercial policy is no longer based on the numbers produced today for tomorrow, but on developing a sales channel'.

Resilient companies have more sophisticated bonus and performance systems based not only on quantitative indicators but also on qualitative components. Increasingly, they work with bonus banks in which variable parts of annual compensation are deferred three to five years (Figure 7.3).

UBS, seeking to increase its level of resilience, launched a bonus bank in 2008 after the Swiss government had guaranteed a bailout of USD 60 billion. E*Trade Financial (ETFC), Charles Schwab (SCHW) and JPMorgan Chase (JPM) have decided to follow the same path. At UBS, bonus banks are structured as follows: one-third of top managers' annual bonuses are paid out and the rest is deposited into an account. The money can be withdrawn after three years (some firms have extended this period to five years or more) provided that the bank obtains or exceeds predetermined targets and goals related to the manager's specific tasks. Otherwise, managers can lose all or part of the deposit. This discourages attitudes focused on profit in a single year at the expense of future profit.

However, the bonus bank is a difficult system to implement. Briggs and Stratton, a US company that manufactures engines for machinery, such as lawn mowers, introduced the bonus bank in the early 1990s. The system

[5] See '2009 Stern Stewart Report' at: www.sternstewart.com/files/ssco_studie31_en.pdf.

worked well until 2005, when a wave of dry weather temporarily reduced demand for the company's products. Although the company was in a good position with respect to its competition, the bonus accounts started to go into the red and managers had to give up a portion of future payments. The bonus bank became a disincentive, such that the board set a cap on bonus-bank losses and introduced a temporary supplementary bonus plan (*Business Week*, 2 March 2009).[6]

DOES YOUR FIRM PLAN FOR THE LONG- TERM?

Our research suggests that the capability to plan for the long-term increases resilience and, in turn, produces sustained superior performance. To assess the extent to which a firm is oriented towards the long term, use this quick test. The various factors can be evaluated on a scale from 1 to 5 (where 1 = strongly disagree and 5 = completely agree) and link to resilience-related actions that can be introduced in the company. Of course, you are free to modify the tool and integrate the short questionnaire with other items or indicators that are already used to measure performance in various areas of the firm.

Table 7.1 **Assess your firm's long-term orientation**

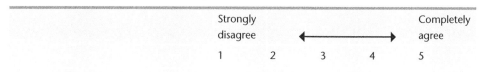

	Strongly disagree				Completely agree
	1	2	3	4	5
My organization identifies trends that may have potential in the long term, while also resolving issues related to current products and services.					
My organization has a formalized process that allows for development of a vision, a long-term strategy for how to get there, and a way for transforming vision and strategy into short-term objectives.					
The actions taken by my company today are aimed at tomorrow's success.					

[6] See 'Executive Pay: Banks Bonus' at: www.businessweek.com/stories/2009-02-03/executive-pay -bonus-banks.

Table 7.1 (cont.)

	Strongly disagree				Completely agree
	1	2	3	4	5
My organization cares about the well-being of its employees and provides incentive systems linked to long-term objectives.					
Long-term orientation score (the average of the four answers)					
Reference grid	1–2: Low resilience. You are not prepared for external shocks and need to invest in a resilience programme.				
	3: Average resilience. Identify blind resilience spots and work on them.				
	4–5: High resilience. Stay the course. Make sure you stay alert.				

Source: Adapted from Shiu, Walsh, Shaw and Hassan (2011).

CHAPTER 8

Process Tools for Supporting Strategic Decision Making

Resilient firms use formal strategic-management processes to complement intuition in decision making. As in the Super Mario video game, where a player can scale numerous levels of difficulty, we seem to have entered a world with a higher level of decision-making difficulty – a world with greater volatility, which forces executives to have better analytical, decision-making and execution skills. Skilled players can guide Super Mario because they have memorized the scenes, and they use their intuition and reflexes to deal with new situations. In business, unfortunately, intuition often leads to flawed decision making. Managers tend to fall into decision-making traps: they prefer recent data, seek confirmation of their own theories or place disproportionate weight on the first pieces of information they receive.

Therefore, a structured approach to decision making is needed to increase the resilience of firms. In the past, it was not only about the speed of decision making but also about timing. Increasingly, however, we see that market volatility forces firms to react quickly. The famous quote from the legendary ice hockey player Wayne Gretzky ('I skate to where the puck is going to be, not where it has been') still applies, but it seems that the game has become harder to predict. Hence, decision-making speed has become one of the main sources of sustainable competitive advantage. As the sociologist Zygmunt Bauman puts it: 'We've gone from a world where big fish ate the little fish to a world where the fast eat the slow (Bauman, 2009).'

There is a trade-off between the speed with which decisions are made and the quality of those decisions (Schweiger, Sandberg and Ragan, 1986). As the former Formula 1 driver Mario Andretti once stated: 'If everything seems under control, you're not going fast enough.' The pressure resulting from time constraints can increase the capacity to process information, but it can also harm performance in the execution of a single task (Perlow, Okhuysen and Repenning, 2002). Bureaucratic red tape or the need to take intermediate steps when the external environment changes very quickly can undermine the opportunity to perform well. Not being able to decide quickly means losing time to market, and inability to keep up with customers' needs or competitors' moves. Therefore, Eisenhardt and Sull (2001) suggest that companies should simplify strategies and absorb market complexity by developing strategies as 'simple rules'.

Simple rules help managers set investment priorities while avoiding a static positioning in given markets or long-term commitments to unique resources. Instead, simple rules help establish strategy processes around promising areas for growth. Such processes may include product innovation, partnering or market entry (Eisenhardt and Sull, 2001, p. 109) with the goal of speeding up these activities. Obviously, market entry requires a certain level of resource commitment and market positioning. However, instead of long processes of analysis (and maybe paralysis), fast companies have standard processes that allow them to determine whether the market is attractive and whether there is potential to gain a significant market share.

This chapter describes why decision making is complex and introduces the strategic process as a method for improving both the speed of decision making and the quality of decisions.

WHY DECISION MAKING IS COMPLEX AND HOW TO REDUCE COMPLEXITY

There are many easy ways to improve strategic decision making in firms. Let us start with some organizational measures. We have identified six main organizational reasons for why decision making in business often requires a great deal of time.

Excessively Large Management Teams

Why have we abandoned the rule of thumb that teams must not exceed eight people? Today, companies often have management teams with ten or more people. In fact, many CEOs have more than twenty direct reports. Until 2012, Mitsubishi had twenty-nine people at the forefront making decisions. Just organizing a face-to-face meeting with twenty-nine people is a complex task, let alone managing the discussion and decision-making process.

The extant literature generally defines efficient teams as including five to eight individuals. An increase in these numbers often leads to higher levels of chaos and a lack of clarity in roles, as well as a slowdown in execution capacity (Mueller, 2012). With high numbers, the effort required to coordinate people increases and decision-making efficiency is reduced.

To get the job done in this increasingly complex scenario, we present five methods[1] that today's most prominent business leaders use to efficiently manage the meeting phase:

★ 'Make it quick!' (Sheryl Sandberg, COO of Facebook): according to recent data,[2] the best meeting length is just over thirty minutes.

★ 'Get it while it's hot!' (Jeff Bezos, CEO of Amazon): by only ordering two pizzas to feed meeting attendees, Bezos has found a way to draw the best-sized crowd to meetings and to limit meeting participants to crucial voices. Analysis paralysis is avoided.

★ 'I'll see you Friday – or – skip it!' (Satya Nadella, CEO of Microsoft): it is useful to meet frequently to coordinate progress. One meeting per week could be a good solution, as is the use of frequent but shorter and smaller meetings. However, it is also useful to save time by avoiding unnecessary meetings and encouraging team members to skip meetings they do not really need to attend.

★ 'No-meeting Wednesdays!' (Facebook's motto): Blue Jeans' data show that the most popular day of the week for a meeting is Tuesday. Wednesday is often viewed as a day dedicated to productive work without interruption.

★ 'Punk-rock style' (CEO of vArmour Networks): the person who calls the meeting has the opportunity to set the tone. 'Punk-rock' meeting management should shake things up with nonconformist ideas. The point is that this is your show.

The right number of members for a team depends on the nature of the work, the extent of skill overlap and the budget. However, 'generally, teams should be fewer than 10 members. It is wise to compose teams using the smallest number of people who can do the task'.[3]

Management Teams with Too Many Generalists

Is it better to have a management team composed of generalists – who basically know a little about a lot of things – or specialists – who know a lot about very little? Based on an analysis of the top management team composition of 160 firms over a period of ten years, we conclude that resilient firms are led by

---

[1] For the full article, see www.huffingtonpost.com/krish-ramakrishnan/from-pizza-to-punk-5 -ways_b_7977790.html.

[2] Blue Jeans State of the Modern Meeting Index.

[3] Hackman (1987).

managers who have specialized in a functional area. If you do not agree with our results, consider the following scenarios. Assume for a minute that your team has been sent on vacation for the next three years and you need to hire a new team. Would you rather recruit specialists or generalists? When a new CEO is appointed for a troubled company, should the supervisory board try to match the profile of potential candidates with the nature of the turnaround challenge? On a similar note, would you recommend that a thirty-year old colleague in your company work on her weaknesses to boost her career or focus on her strengths to develop signature skills?

The inclusion of specialists on your team has many advantages. If all team members know a little about everything, it becomes difficult to make decisions. A team of generalists is a team of people with extensive knowledge, but that knowledge is not necessarily focused on the business or the industry in which it operates. A high number of generalists in a team signals that you are likely to be competent in everything. However, when decisions have to be made quickly, you might discover that your team does not excel at anything. The well-known expression 'Jack of all trades and master of none' is appropriate in this context (Buyl et al., 2011). The inclusion of skills that are too extended often means a trend towards superficiality. When decisions need to be made quickly but the knowledge to make them is likely, delays and inefficiencies result. Executive board members therefore need to have signature skills and knowledge that accelerates the decision-making process.

Using Complexity as an Excuse

Even if the decision-making elements have increased and become more dynamic in their interactions, complexity is too often used as an excuse for a lack of decision making. The complexity of the environment and the interactions needed to arrive at a decision are highly evident, especially because the need to manage huge quantities of structured and unstructured data is increasingly common (i.e. big data management). Complexity is a challenge that entails acquiring or developing tools that enable simplification. Often, however, it becomes an excuse for doing nothing: 'How can we operate with all this bureaucracy?' 'Why make a decision when we know that nothing will happen?' and 'In our company, discussions start after a decision is made.'

If we add the many incentives focused on short-term performance (e.g. linked to bonus and career progress) to this perceived increase in complexity, one can understand why it has become increasingly difficult for management teams to make strategic decisions. What manager will make decisions with long-term effects for the benefit of successors if those effects reduce current performance? Too often, companies are oriented towards short-term results and concerned with plugging holes, and therefore lose sight of what might happen in the near future. This is why the first investments that are usually cut are in training, R & D, marketing and advertising. It is also for this reason that employee incentives are designed for the short term. This type of vision is short-sighted and leads to inconsistent decisions.

Weak Supervisory Boards

A well-structured supervisory board can accelerate decisions and improve their quality. Resilient firms have supervisory boards composed of members that think like owners. This is a prerequisite for being able to effectively influence the CEO and the management board, and to ensure that their interests match those of the owners. Too often, we find disengaged board members who know little about the company and its business challenges. To make firms more resilient, strong supervisory boards are key.

In this regard, family firms can learn from the practices of the leading listed firms. Again, some boards are too large. How can you have effective conversations with more than fifteen board members? Especially in a highly political context with high information asymmetry between managers and owners' representatives, it is essential to have stable boards that develop a common language for strategy and investment decisions, and feel comfortable challenging ideas. One way to make large boards more effective is to create supervisory board committees, usually for strategy, compensation and technology. The required qualifications of board members have to be defined accordingly. If your company increasingly faces competition in commodity-type markets, you want to have someone with experience in that area. Similarly, if your long-term growth strategy requires the creation and management of joint-venture structures in emerging markets, it would help to have a board member with experience in that field. Obviously, weak CEOs will fear losing power and decision speed, but powerful supervisory boards can substantially enhance the quality of strategic decisions – especially in a truly public company with a dispersed shareholder structure.

On how many supervisory boards can a single person serve? We have met seasoned managers who were members of more than thirty supervisory boards. They were probably selected for these boards because of their networks and their prestige. However, can they really add value? If they participate in supervisory board meetings, they often do so via conference call. In our view, it makes little sense to have disengaged board members who receive a relatively small payment of EUR 10,000–20,000 per year for participation in four to ten meetings per year. In theory, the supervisory board should approve the strategy and main investments proposed by the CEO. What is the minimum level of engagement that a supervisory board member needs to have to be able to close the information gap and to constructively challenge the business plan proposed by the management?

Boards of directors often meet because they have to, but these meetings are not exploited to the fullest. Careful planning of the meeting's objectives, the needs that need to be met and the best way of organizing the meeting (where, when, with what agenda) allows optimization of the meeting and facilitates decision making.

Inability to Deal with Decision Biases

> One thing after another pleases then troubles us, because our judgements are not only incorrect but also fickle.
>
> (Seneca)

Decision making requires following a logical path that others can easily understand. In other words, complexity must be confronted with a method. Only the careful planning of issues and future actions can simplify strategic decisions and enable effective communications with everyone in the company. The study of decision making dates back to the early 1950s (Edwards, 1954). The application of psychology to the study of decisions was initiated by such scholars as Tversky, Slovic, Lichtenstein and Kahneman in the 1960s and 1970s (Kahneman and Tversky, 1979; Lichtenstein and Slovic, 1971, Tversky, 1969). Theory has highlighted how decisions based on heuristics lead to decisional errors.

Managers can be subject to numerous evaluation errors. One is deciding on the basis of intuition: rational and objective elements are often not carefully considered when attempting to arrive at a decision, as people prefer to act according to a 'sixth sense' or intuition. In particular, Mintzberg (1975) found that managers are likely to use intuition in their decision making. Isenberg (1984), who studied the decisions of twelve experienced managers for two years, believed that they rarely used analytical decision procedures but preferred to trust their intuition. At times, intuition can yield excellent results, but it can also lead to disastrous outcomes.

The outcomes of decisions are subject to unknown and high risk factors. One risk factor is that humans base their decisions on past experience. Managers try to assess the current situation in light of their past experiences. This leads them to use the same criteria as those used in similar situations in the past without considering the fact that each decision is different and may have different effects. If relying on past experience is paired with a tendency to seek confirmation of one's own theories, decisions may be flawed. We naturally attribute more importance to affirmations than negations. Information is selected in such a way as to focus greater attention on – and therefore give greater credibility to – aspects that confirm our beliefs. Conversely, we tend to ignore or belittle information that contradicts those beliefs. This may lead to confirmation of a theory even when that theory is false.

We also tend to analyse the past with greater indulgence, and we are inclined to judge an event in retrospect. After an event, people may wrongly believe that they should have been able to correctly predict that event. Moreover, people tend to believe that the past was better than it really was. This leads to an underestimation of the weight of decisions to be made in the present and to a belief that a decision is simpler than it actually is.

The following table summarizes the main decision biases.

Table 8.1 Biases and managerial implications

Bias	Definition	Business examples
Anchorage	In the face of incomplete or ambiguous information, individuals often use information that is immediately available as an anchor or reference point. A classic example is that of an item on sale in a shop: we tend to evaluate and consider the price difference between two objects on display, but not the absolute price of the item.	A seller plans future product sales by looking only at data for past sales. In a market that evolves quickly, forecasting ability can be compromised.
Availability	The availability heuristic estimates the probability of an event based on the availability of information in memory and the emotional impact of the memory, rather than on the true objective probability that the event in question will occur. The more the information is visible, known and available, the more it is thought to be relevant.	A classic example is that of advertising. A commercial repeated several times on television is imprinted in the mind and induces consumers to search for that brand in the purchasing phase.

Table 8.1 (cont.)

Bias	Definition	Business examples
Representativeness	We tend to attribute similar characteristics to similar objects. This similarity may be due to the fact that the objects share some superficial characteristics or that there is a causal relationship between them. Kahneman and Tversky (1979) identified this heuristic through an experiment. A group of individuals were shown two sequences of coin flips and had to decide which was the most likely: (a) H - H - H - H - T - T - T - T or (b) H - H - T - H - T - T - H - T. After seeing the two sequences, the majority of individuals chose option (b) as the most probable because the irregular intervals of H (heads) and T (tails) appear to be more likely than the perfectly ordered sequence of case 'a'. In fact, both sequences have the same probability of occurring because the events (the coin flips) are mutually independent. By the same reasoning, people who play roulette think that if the ball has stopped on red several consecutive times, then it will inevitably stop on black next.	A manager assessing the performance of his employees may attribute greater weight to what those employees did in the previous period.
Confirmation bias	Individuals search for or interpret information in a way that confirms their initial opinion without incurring changes. Indeed, we tend to prefer associating with others with similar tastes and points of view, or reading newspapers that are on the same political side.	A CEO who is considering cancelling the expansion of a plant may seek advice from a friend who has just decided not to proceed with the expansion of his plant.
Sunk cost	People sometimes make decisions that favour erroneous past decisions. In other words, sunk costs describes an error that is pursued when the individual decides to continue to invest in something even if it turns out to be a bad investment. The decision maker falls into this trap because he hopes to remedy the negativity of the moment and be able to uncover a positive outcome. This is why we sometimes repair an old car even when we know that it would be better to buy a new one, or why we invest in relationships that are not working in the hope of saving them.	A bank that already has problems related to loans may continue to lend to borrowers in order to offset past decisions.

Table 8.1 (cont.)

Bias	Definition	Business examples
Status quo	Events happening in the present moment become a barrier to change. Change is frightening, and we try to keep things as they are.	The status quo bias leads to a love of routines, certain foods and favourite places. The most damaging part of this bias is the unwarranted assumption that a different choice could make things worse.

Source: Adapted from Hammond, Keeney and Raiffa (2006).

Decision making is complex, but there are useful tools to help make high-quality decisions quickly. The strategic process described in the following section allows managers to overcome some elements of complexity in business decision making and to avoid decision biases.

QUICK DECISION MAKING REQUIRES PLANNING

Some argue that given the complexity of the external environment, we should no longer think in terms of strategic planning. Each step in a company's strategy appears to evolve to a degree that would suggest continuous and flexible adaptation in search of an ever-transitional advantage (McGrath, 2013). Leaders may therefore choose to skip 'good processes' and simply act according to a trial and error logic. In other words, they may follow their whims: 'behaving capriciously signals and may even create the power that leaders crave – and that they often need to effect valuable change. But it also takes its toll on employees and potentially undermines organisational performance (Pfeffer, 2013). Our research suggests that relying solely on the CEO's 'gut feeling' or on pure luck to accommodate continuous changes in the market seldom leads to a successful strategy. Moreover, in such cases, a superior strategy is unlikely to be subsequently created.

Strategic planning is very useful and relevant precisely because there are many variables to consider. If a strategy is not implemented methodologically, major mistakes can be made.

Raoul Ascari, COO of SACE, a global leader in credit insurance and investment protection, said: 'what I explain to my co-workers is that our operations are complex. The challenge is finding someone who takes this complexity, is able to take apart all of its elements and knows how to re-assemble them in an orderly manner. Even complex tasks lead to decisions. Sometimes we make the right decisions. Sometimes we make mistakes. The difficulty we have

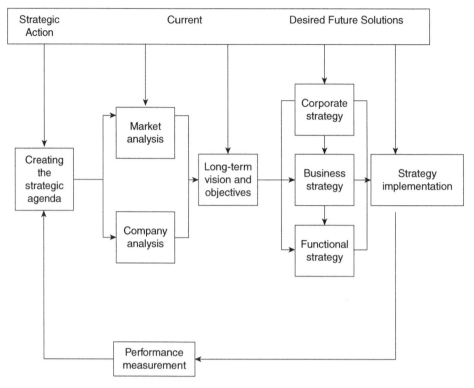

Figure 8.1 The strategic process
Source: Venzin (2005)

is methodological'. In tackling strategic issues, frameworks like the one proposed below help reduce complexity and develop actionable strategies.

If the variables increase in number, the best way to analyse them is by creating options, ordering them and then considering them one at a time. The strategic process is a scheme that allows implementation of this simplification and reasoning. It starts with identification of strategic business issues and includes determining the actions that can be used to implement the strategy. The intermediate steps are those that consider the key elements of the market and the company, and attempt to develop a vision for the future. In other words, we suggest proceeding methodically and in subsequent steps. The strategic challenges are put in order according to their importance and urgency, thereby creating a true strategic agenda. This strategic agenda allows for the business priorities to be defined. The subsequent analysis of the current and the desired situations allows for planning of the necessary actions.

Therefore, a tool that simplifies the transition from planning to implementation is essential for companies wishing to increase their resilience. This is even truer for multinational companies. In fact, companies need a system that can grasp the often innovative and creative ideas of talented people within and outside the organization at both the central and peripheral levels. Carlsberg serves as an example of a company that, by formulating a strategic plan, has succeeded in improving relations between the parent company and its subsidiaries. In 2010, the local market offices were asked to develop a three-year strategic plan based on some strategic issues. The objectives were to build dialogue between local organizations and regional management team, and to encourage long-term strategic planning. In addition, Carlsberg harmonized the strategic-planning process by introducing a formal strategic process with systematized parts and a common strategic framework known as the 'strategy development toolkit'. The strategic process was designed to tie the strategic planning in the spring with the financial planning in the autumn with a view to establishing a dialogue among different group offices. In addition, the toolkit was sent to all of the CEOs of the local markets and to the top management team. This created a shared language and a common starting point for the formulation of strategy within the group. In the following two years, the strategy process was updated and improved based on feedback received from the various local offices.

ORGANIZING STRATEGIC WORKSHOPS TO ENABLE PLANNING

To enable good and quick decision making, managers need to learn how to organize strategic workshops. Although opinions can be expressed in informal meetings, thoughts may remain unstructured and collective decision making may be difficult. Formal meetings can be used to codify strategic thinking, allocate resources to various initiatives and institutionalize strategic decisions that may have been made in informal settings. We call these meetings 'strategic workshops'. When strategic workshops are well organized, swift and high-quality decisions can be achieved.

On a scale from 1 (not at all) to 10 (very much), how satisfied are you with your current strategy meetings? We have the impression that most managers are reasonably good at running meetings that cover short-term operational issues. However, when they are called on to organize a strategy workshop, many of them fail miserably.

There are many different types of strategy workshops, each of which is subject to different problems. They include:

★ *Visioning exercise:* a group (usually large and diverse) meets to discuss strategy, often in broad terms (e.g. where should our company be in five years?).

★ *Formal annual planning meetings:* these annual meetings are part of the strategic-planning process (e.g. where a business unit or division presents its proposed strategy to the corporate centre).

★ *Ad-hoc strategy meetings:* these meetings are held to decide on a strategic response to a specific issue (e.g. market-entry strategy of division A in country B). They are often a follow-up to a 'deep' investigation by a task force.

★ *Board meetings:* in these meetings, a firm seeks approval for the corporate strategic plan, or a specific strategic decision and corresponding investment (e.g. acquisition of company A).

Now, let us look at frequently heard complaints (FHCs) about strategy workshops that start out as visioning exercises and some ideas for addressing them:

★ *FHC 1:* 'We start the workshop with the intention of talking about strategic issues, but we are soon discussing operational issues.' – Suggestion: separate strategy meetings from operational meetings by time and space. It is very hard to switch to issues that are not urgent but have a high impact if you are pressured by day-to-day issues.

★ *FHC 2:* 'We tried to tackle too many issues.' – Suggestion: concentrate on a few 'must-win-battles' that have been identified through a visioning exercise and prioritized using an urgency/impact matrix.

★ *FHC 3:* 'Our discussions are tainted by political games regarding how to slice the pie.' – Suggestion: clearly state that the objective is to enlarge the pie. Manage power games by identifying a moderator, assigning individual or group tasks or creating conversational rules. Conversational rules, in particular, can change the dynamics of strategy workshops. Such rules can be simple, like 'be on time' or 'turn off your phones'. However, they may also include more complex rules, like 'respect individual opinions' or 'do not intimidate others'.

★ *FHC 4:* 'I did not understand much of what was said.' – Suggestion: stable teams that frequently meet face-to-face create a common language for strategy. Try this test: write down the ten key concepts that you use most often (e.g. 'relevant market share', 'strategic clients' or 'core technology') and ask members of your management team to individually define the elements of those concepts. The variety of interpretations are likely to surprise you.

★ *FHC 5:* 'We seem to always discuss the same issues.' – Suggestion: strategy meetings should be decision oriented. By distributing pre-meeting reading material that is categorized as 'for information', 'for discussion' or 'for decision', everyone knows what is going to happen in the meeting. Too often, 'discussions start with a decision', so be sure to stick with well-prepared and discussed decisions once they are made.

★ *FHC 6:* 'We did not have enough information to make decisions.' – Suggestion: if you still feel that you do not have enough information to make a decision, it may be because your management team is composed of too many generalists who 'know a little about everything'. You may need some functional specialists who 'know everything about nothing'. Also, management team members should involve their teams in preparing for the strategy workshop to ensure that decisions are based on a broad set of experiences and to facilitate strategy execution.

★ *FHC 7:* 'We just engaged in a brainstorming exercise.' – Suggestion: brainstorming is a creativity methodology that can be applied for five to ten minutes. By inviting participants to a brainstorming session on the company's future, you signal that you did not have enough time to properly prepare for the meeting.

★ *FHC 8:* 'Too many people are invited.' – Suggestion: reduce the core strategy team to five to eight people. If your management team is larger, work with sub-groups. The formal, annual strategy process usually involves several teams: a core team that meets weekly (i.e. CEO with direct reports), a management committee of up to twenty-five people that meets on a quarterly basis (i.e. core team plus managers representing the second dimension of the matrix organization) and a senior management meeting that occurs once per year (i.e. top 100–200 in the firm).

★ *FHC 9:* 'There is little communication between our strategy exercise and the budget or our individual goals.' – Suggestion: the broad vision that depicts the company in five to ten years should be translated into three-year financial plans before the budgeting process begins. These medium-term plans build the basis for the ensuing years' financial ambitions, which are then used to construct individual goals and bonus schemes.

★ *FHC 10:* 'The next steps are not clear.' – Suggestion: ensure that someone is taking notes and codifying the workshop results. Ideally, decisions will be made during the workshops, but there will most likely be some issues that need further analysis. As a closing exercise in the workshop, create a strategy-project portfolio with project leaders, goals and timelines. Set a date for another strategy meeting in six to eight weeks, at which decisions are to be made concerning these issues.

This is only a selection of the complaints that frustrated managers have when they leave strategy meetings. The systematic collection of feedback after strategy workshops can help improve their quality. This is how management teams can develop one of the last sources of sustainable competitive advantage: the ability to have productive conversations about the future that lead to sound strategic decisions. The following section discusses the main design elements of strategic workshops.

The Participants

The complexity of selecting participants for a strategic workshop is reminiscent of preparing wedding invitations. Managers should try to avoid political mistakes by inviting the right people, but they should also select a small number of participants. In terms of the strategic-management process, managers should bear in mind that both political aspects and knowledge play crucial roles. In addition, they should remember that, at times, even actors outside the company (e.g. unhappy customers or operators of an outsourced call centre) can be invited. If the invite list includes ten or more people, smaller subgroups can be formed during the workshop. The diversity and geographical distance of the top management team may be one element of difficulty for multinational companies. Ideally, the strategy should be developed by a stable team whose members can frequently interact.

To reduce the number of participants in a strategy workshop, some multinationals may categorize markets into three classes: A = high volume and a large market share, B = lower volume but growing, and C = low volume but future potential. Often, only managers from class-A markets are invited, while those from classes B and C are forced to endure the choices made by others. This type of classification can be useful if resources need to be allocated, but is not appropriate for organizing strategic workshops. Classes B and C are often more distant, and their market conditions differ from those of the central market. Therefore, an understanding of their needs can be useful. Rather than having direct interaction with headquarters, the creation of regional headquarters can help manage the increasing complexity associated with market diversity.

The Location

The workshop should preferably be organized offsite in order to have as few interruptions or distractions as possible. In addition, a change of environment could have the effect of inspiring and relaxing participants, thereby reducing the risk of power games. In any case, the choice of location must be made intelligently. For example, a workshop on cost savings should not be held in a five-star hotel. If possible, participants should spend at least one night at the selected location, which facilitates team spirit and creates greater flexibility in the use of time. Many multinational companies support the idea of respecting local differences by choosing a different subsidiary each year as the venue for their meetings.

Preparatory Phase

In multinationals, involving the middle management of subsidiaries in a workshop's preparatory work is essential. All too often, managers of local offices participate in a two-day workshop and return home with only a faint idea of the group's strategy and the implications for their businesses. They are often not in a position to articulate the group's goals and purposes, or the nature of the competitive advantage. An explicit communication plan that attempts to involve all managers of subsidiary offices is essential. The workshop invitation should include the topics that will be discussed and an indication of how individual participants should be prepared. In addition, the classification of documents according to three categories of importance can help hard-pressed managers set priorities:

★ *For information*: information documents are useful as base material. They help managers understand the context in which strategic decisions are being made.
★ *For discussion*: these documents should be read if participants are an active part of what is taking place in the workshop. If managers do not take the time to read these documents, they cannot actively participate in the discussion.
★ *For decisions*: a good strategic workshop is oriented towards decision making. Managers know that a series of strategic decisions will be made during the workshop. If they do not read the relevant documents, they automatically lose their right to vote.

The preparatory phase can help managers focus on present and past decisions, and not only on the final analyses. This helps ensure that strategic meetings are based on past meetings. Many large companies suffer from 'analysis paralysis', while smaller and more agile companies have a competitive edge from this point of view.

Timing

In many large multinationals, the annual formal planning process (Figure 8.2) is well organized and starts with the development of a corporate strategy at the headquarters level in February (assuming that the fiscal year ends on 31 December). At this stage, decisions are made that affect the general distribution of resources among the various business units and the achievement of synergies among different areas. The business strategy meetings at the subsidiary level usually start around the month of May with the aim of producing a long-term business plan. Business plans are transformed into three-year or medium-term plans, and they are not necessarily revised each year. Many companies undertake the full-year strategic exercise every third year, adjusting only parts of the plan in the intervening two years. Towards the end of the year, medium-term plans serve as the basis for preparing the budget, which is typically followed by individual meetings on achieving the targets in January/February (management by objectives, or MBO).

There are different types of models. The one shown above is often used by multinationals that have prominent central offices and top-down power. In addition to these formal models, more informal mechanisms can be

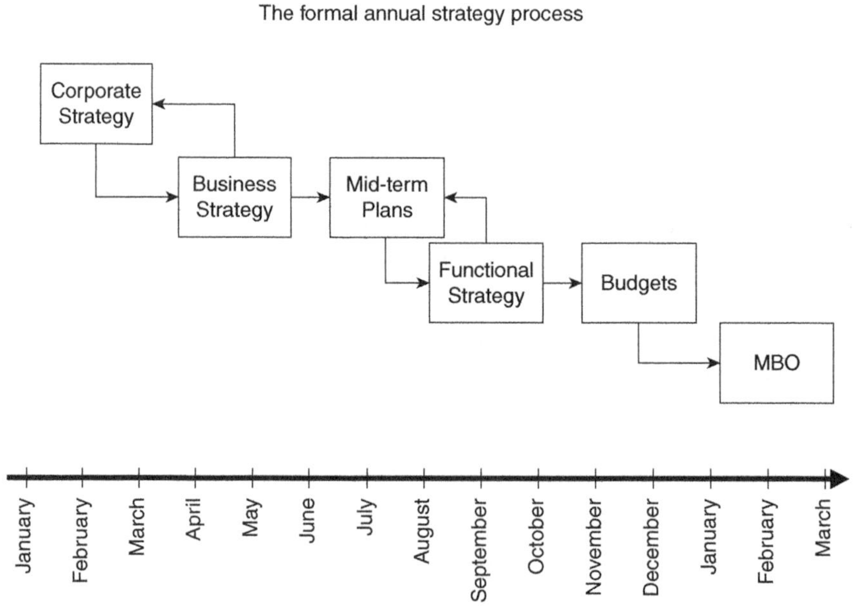

The formal annual strategy process

Figure 8.2 Formal annual planning
Source: Venzin (2005)

employed. If a competitor unexpectedly launches a new product in July, immediate measures must be discussed and organized to establish a response strategy. Informal mechanisms are often more important than formal mechanisms, especially in large companies where making joint decisions on a regular basis is difficult. Multinational companies use social-control mechanisms (the opposite of a bureaucratic system) based on shared values, norms and informal relationships to steer strategy processes. Nevertheless, the formal strategy workshop itself serves to legitimize decisions and allocate resources to official strategic projects.

Programme

The strategic process can be used to structure the strategic workshop. Strategic workshops usually last for two or three days. They can start, for example, at 4.00 p.m. on a Thursday afternoon with a welcome coffee, followed by a short keynote speech by the head of the unit, who highlights the main objectives of the workshop. An introductory session aimed at explaining the basic concepts of the strategy can be useful if the team is not familiar with the strategic terms.

Standardized language should be used in the workshop, especially if there are major cultural differences. To ensure detachment from everyday activities and foster team spirit, participants can use the rest of Thursday as leisure time. Alternatively, participants could be engaged in group exercises designed to identify the company's vision (see Box 8.1). The actual work could then start on Friday.

This is only one way of starting a workshop. It is important to create an atmosphere of sharing and creativity at the beginning of the session. Experience shows that it takes at least half a day for participants to feel involved in a workshop and for their minds to shift away from everyday tasks.

Moderator

The moderator's role should be assigned to a capable manager. The role of the moderator is to guide the workshop, structure the discussion and enforce deadlines. In general, this activity is not directly linked to content.

However, moderators should interact with participants based on their strategic skills and respect for cultural differences. Moderators may be external consultants, internal members of the organization or members of the top management team.

Box 8.1 Group activities designed to identify the corporate vision

1 For group activities, five teams can be formed. Each team is assigned a different function: team 1 represents a supplier, team 2 represents the competitors, team 3 represents the media, team 4 serves as the top management team and team 5 adopts the consumer perspective.

2 The teams are invited to write a short article for the company's internal newspaper dated July 2023. The article is entitled 'I did not think it would happen... the company I would like'. The article is to optimistically envisage the wonderful results that the company has produced and the internal processes that have been put in place to achieve that performance.

3 The teams write the article as if they were in the future but the article should be written in the present tense.

4 The next morning, the teams read their articles to the other workshop participants without immediately receiving comments. This allows the different teams to develop a perception of how the company's future could be.

5 A list of strategic priorities is drawn up in accordance with the articles. The choice of themes becomes the starting point for subsequent steps in the strategic process (e.g. market analysis, company analysis).

Results

The main results are usually put in writing. This helps ensure that the strategic workshop is based on those already organized by the company in the past. At the end of the workshop, participants should feel that they have produced something tangible. The use of the strategic process within the workshop can be extremely helpful in this regard. A written sequential schema can be compiled that provides legible, easily communicable output on a single sheet.

HOW GOOD IS YOUR FIRM AT MAKING STRATEGIC DECISIONS?

Our research suggests that the capability to plan for the long-term increases resilience and, in turn, produces sustained superior performance. To assess the extent to which a firm is oriented towards the long term, use this quick test. The various factors can be evaluated on a scale from 1 to 5 (where 1 = strongly disagree and 5 = completely agree) and relate to the resilience-related actions that can be introduced in the company. Of course, you are free to modify the tool and integrate the short questionnaire with other items or indicators that are already used to measure performance in various areas of the firm.

Table 8.2 Assess your firm's decision-making capability

	Strongly disagree ⟵———⟶ Completely agree				
	1	2	3	4	5
In my organization, decisions are often made quickly and lead to good results.					
In my organization, regular meeting opportunities, such as task groups or committees, are available to discuss strategic issues.					
The strategy is discussed among middle and upper managers, and everyone's opinion is taken into consideration. However, in the end, one or two people make the final decision.					
When dealing with a strategic theme, models and written procedures are used.					
Decision-making capability score (the average of the four answers)					
Reference grid	1–2: Low resilience. You are not prepared for external shocks and need to invest in a resilience programme.				
	3: Average resilience. Identify blind resilience spots and work on them.				
	4–5: High resilience. Stay the course. Make sure you stay alert.				

Source: Adapted from Thomas and McDaniel (1990).

CHAPTER 9

Ownership Structure, Span of Control and Organizational Design

Choices linked to organizational design, such as the simplification of processes, the strengthening of social control, or the size and composition of top management teams, have a significant effect on the resilience of companies because they shape the way that people interact. Ultimately, it is the people who make a company more or less resilient. This chapter explores the last driver in our resilience model: ownership structure and top management team (TMT) composition, and the organizational-design decisions that have an impact on their effectiveness. We start off with a discussion of the impact of ownership structure on TMTs because we believe that the radical change processes that firms need to set up when faced with a crisis are most likely initiated at the top. We then discuss the optimal size for TMTs, and whether their members should be specialists or generalists.

OWNERSHIP STRUCTURE[1]

The management literature suggests that the ownership structure has a major impact on TMTs and, ultimately, the performance of a firm. To address the relationships among ownership structure, sustainable superior performance and resilience, we analysed the relevant literature, and we drew on a broad and diverse empirical base that comprised both primary data (234 listed companies in the automotive, pharmaceutical and banking industries; interviews with senior managers; and company documents) and secondary sources (case studies, research papers and newspaper articles). This is only a preliminary analysis, but by thinking through the following claims, we hope to facilitate the discussion of the impact of ownership structure on the resilience of firms.

---

[1] The authors thank Niccolò Bongiachino for his contribution to this section.

Claim 1: Widely Held Companies Are Less Resilient than Companies with a Controlling Shareholder

The topic of ownership concentration and its influence on organizational behaviour and corporate performance has been widely analysed. Most of the literature focuses on the implications of ownership concentration for share-holders' contributions to the company and suggests that a highly concentrated structure solves or at least reduces the agency problem that arises from the separation of property and control. Therefore, ownership concentration is viewed as an effective governance mechanism that reduces the likelihood of managerial opportunism, and unethical or illegal behaviour (Shleifer and Vishny, 1997). The fundamental problem with diffused ownership is that a joint owner does not have the same incentives as either a manager or a sole owner. The more fractured the ownership, the greater this free-rider problem. In our research, we noted substantial differences in ownership concentration across geographies. Diffused ownership is more common in the United States than in Europe. As a consequence, shareholders tend to be more active in the United States than in Europe. The pressure that CEOs in the United States feel from well-organized shareholder activists is considerably higher than in Europe, especially as management compensation has risen and top salaries are paid even if the company is not creating value for shareholders.

Nevertheless, minority shareholders generally do not have the same attitude towards management supervision and the goal of creating sustained superior performance (SSP) as majority shareholders. The incentive to voice concerns over the firm's strategic and operational decisions is often lower for minority shareholders, and the costs they would incur in monitoring outweigh the potential gains. These shareholders might rationally decide to behave as free riders and benefit from the supervision of larger investors. Shareholders with significant ownership stakes may influence, either directly or indirectly, firm decisions, such as the selection of members of the board or the appointment of the CEO. Moreover, they have the capabilities needed to efficiently and effectively undertake monitoring by leveraging on proprietary industry insights and specific company knowledge. In this way, they are able to minimize information asymmetries, which are at the root of agency costs.

We therefore suggest that a concentrated ownership structure reduces the misalignment between property and control that is typical of listed corporations. Controlling shareholders ensure that their actions are aimed at delivering SSP. This finding is in line with research suggesting that ownership concentration positively affects company performance and market value (Alimehmeti and Paletta, 2012; Gedajlovic and Shapiro, 2002).

Claim 2: Family-controlled Firms Are More Resilient than Non-family Firms

In a family-owned company, one or more family members are directly involved in the management of the business, and the majority of ownership or control lies within the family (Gubitta and Giannecchini, 2002. Such family firms can reach a considerable size, especially in emerging economies. Examples of large family-owned firms include the Tata Group in India (controlled by the Tata family; the group's twenty-four listed companies represent almost 7.8 per cent of the Bombay Stock Exchange's total market capitalization), the Koc Group in Turkey (controlled by the Koc family; 2015 market capitalization of more than EUR 10 billion) and the Carso Group in Mexico (controlled by Carlos Slim; 2015 market capitalization of more than EUR 75 billion). It is relatively easier for family firms to reach this size and importance in emerging economies for several reasons:

1   Access to capital and institutional networks are key assets for competing in these markets.
2   Higher environmental uncertainties (i.e. political, government policy, macroeconomic, social, natural) and trade barriers make it difficult for foreign companies to compete.
3   The transaction costs associated with finding business partners and negotiating/reinforcing contracts are high.
4   Market growth is high.

About 90 per cent of all the firms in North America and an even a greater proportion in the developing countries are family owned (Kontinen and Ojala, 2012). There are several well-researched advantages associated with a TMT reporting to a family owner, such as long-term orientation, flexibility, speedy decision making and a family culture, which provides a sense of pride and commitment to the company (Zahra, 2003). Nevertheless, some critical issues need to be considered. For example, attracting and retaining non-family employees can be harder because they may do not wish to deal with family conflicts. Potential employees may think that there are limited opportunities for advancement due to the special treatment sometimes accorded to family members. Moreover, family companies have to deal with 'generational shifts' – determining who will take over leadership and ownership of the company when the current generation retires. Most of these considerations are equally valid in cases in which the controlling shareholder is a single individual.

Given these characteristics, are family firms generally more resilient? Examples like Beiersdorf and Ferrero demonstrate that strong family control positively affects organizational resilience. Beiersdorf, which is famous for its lead brand Nivea and known for other brands like Eucerin, La Prairie, Labello, Atrix, Hansaplast and Tesa, spent several years as a potential takeover target. It was acquired in 2003 by the Herz family of Germany, which also owned Tchibo. Beiersdorf has many of the features of resilient firms discussed in this book: a long-term orientation, product focus, customer centricity and a relatively small TMT that has been recently enlarged to a (still small) group of seven members. Also striking is the recent decision to appoint China's Zhengrong Liu as head of human resources (including the functions of corporate communications, sustainability and labour relations). This move shows the willingness of Beiersdorf to integrate different cultures and pay attention to strategically important markets.

Michele Ferrero, who is famous for inventing Ferrero Rocher and Nutella, died in 2015 at the age of 89. In some ways, he was the archetypical family businessman. He was reluctant to give interviews to the press and often refused to ask consultants for advice, as he was convinced that he knew his business better than anyone else. A long-term orientation is what characterizes Ferrero: 'We were born as a family business and we intend to remain that way,' said Mr Ferrero. 'We are not interested in maximizing revenues in the short term like everyone else. If we were listed, we would be under short-term pressure to deliver dividends and profits.'[2] In addition, Ferrero has a balanced internationalization strategy and a good management team made up of just five members.

Family firms are often believed to outperform non-family firms in terms of financial performance. In their examination of different firms, Sirmon and Hitt (2003) found four key resources – human capital, social capital, patient financial capital and survivability capital – and one governance-related attribute that provide family companies with potential advantages over non-family firms. Human capital represents the acquired knowledge, skills and capabilities of a person that allow for unique and novel actions (Coleman, 1988). Family members are not only extremely committed to the firm, but they also have deep and specific knowledge of it. Social capital is developed

[2] For the full article, see: www.wsj.com/articles/SB10001424052702303559504579200052948857542.

in relationships between individuals and between organizations. Moreover, family firms are considered to be relatively risk averse. Often, the family's investments are not well diversified and tend to be concentrated in the family firm. We agreed that it is easier for some family firms to create resilience simply because they do not have pressure from shareholders to create short-term profits, and because their management teams generally have longer tenures and a desire to hand over a healthy firm to the next generation.

Our results suggest that family-controlled firms are indeed more resilient than non-family firms. The unique ownership structure of family businesses gives them a long-term orientation that is hard to find elsewhere. Kachaner et al. (2012) find that family-controlled firms are prevalent among companies with more than USD 1 billion in sales. This study provides an empirical explanation for their success: family firms are better able to minimize the negative impact of adverse situations and quickly recover when those adverse situations come to an end. Their cautious attitude towards risky investments, which might harm short-term profits, improves performance in the medium to long term and reduces company exposure in the contraction phases of the business cycle.

Claim 3: State Control Has No Significant Impact on the Resilience of Firms

National and local governments often have holdings in listed companies. This is particularly likely if the company operates in an industry that is viewed as strategic (e.g. financial services, energy or telecommunication). Public institutions tend to affect the governance of these companies in two main ways: they redirect the attention of top managers towards objectives that are not purely financial, such as offering services in segments that are not profitable or employment security, and they sometimes defend 'national' control by discouraging potential takeovers by foreign entities. The relationship between government shareholdings and company performance has long been an issue of interest, especially among policymakers. The topic returned to the limelight after the outbreak of the 2008 financial crisis, during which governments and public institutions around the world acquired controlling stakes in many companies that were close to bankruptcy.

Given the high rigidity that often afflicts state-controlled companies and the organizational ambiguity that emerges from the coexistence of economic and policy/political goals, one might expect resilience to be negatively affected by state control. However, our preliminary findings highlighted no significant relationship between governmental control and company resilience. On the one hand, governmental shareholding supports stronger monitoring of managerial activity and firms might benefit from favourable regulations (Tian, 2001). On the other hand, policy objectives linked to non-financial goals can conflict with corporate objectives of profit maximization.

Claim 4: Firms That Are Controlled by Institutional Investors Are More Resilient than Widely Held Firms

Banks, holding companies, pension funds and investment companies are examples of institutional investors. They often provide capital and contribute to the surveillance of management decisions through various governance systems (Zahra et al., 2000). Their decisions have a significant influence on the stock market's movements and, conventionally, they have a significant impact on the corporate affairs of the firms in which they invest. In most cases, institutional investors face fewer protective regulations because they are assumed to be more knowledgeable and better able to protect their interests.

Institutional investors are evaluated regularly on the basis of their financial results. For this reason, they are likely to be very concerned with shareholders' value creation and have developed effective monitoring capabilities over time. For example, the system of relationships between banks and companies is traditionally viewed as one of the main success factors of German industrialization and a distinguishing aspect of national capitalism. Typically, institutional investors contribute to the success of the firms they control through the input of managerial competences and the provision of debt capital.

Hence, institutional investors' control has a positive impact on the ability of a company to deliver SSP. Institutional investors are highly specialized operators that have developed a specific expertise in monitoring the firms in which they hold shares. Their relentless focus on shareholder value maximization, together with their ability to minimize information asymmetries, explains their positive impact on the resilience of controlled companies.

SPAN OF CONTROL

In addition to ownership structure, we investigate the span of control and its effects on resilience. We believe that a wide span of control – a high number of people reporting to a particular supervisor – is one reason why firms become fragile. The broader the span, the more distance is created among people in an organization. Studies have shown that as span of control increases, so does the summoning of individual subordinates to correct unwanted or inappropriate behaviour. A manager with many subordinates spends less time interacting with each of them and is quicker to dismiss them (Kipnis and Lane, 1982).

Our findings indicate that resilient companies are increasingly moving in the direction of simplifying their organizational structures and reducing the number of subordinates without losing the reins of control or running the risk of anarchy. Resilient companies have six to ten first-line managers directly reporting to the CEO. Bharti Airtel, for example, has recently reduced the number of first-line managers from fourteen to seven. The market director of Haier Italy and Greece says: 'We only have five first-line executives. This lean structure allows flexibility and speed of management, and enables us to adapt to changing market conditions in real time.' Similarly, the TMT of Sonepar, a French electrical equipment distributor with more than EUR 16 billion in revenue in 2013, is composed of eight members. Sonepar has identified eight as the ideal team size and compares it to the scrum that is used in rugby.

A scrum is composed of eight players per team who are arranged to form two opposing sides to win possession of a ball, which is put into play into the middle of the scrum by the scrum half. The sides meet in shoulder to shoulder contact. The eight players are arranged in three lines. The front row is composed of two props and a hooker at the centre. This line comes into contact with the first line of opponents. The second row is formed by two players (or locks) who underpin the front row, pushing into the two spaces between the three front-row players. Finally, the third row consists of three players (two flankers and the scrum half) who are the links between the forwards and the backs. The scrum action ends when the ball – without the use of hands – emerges from the back of the scrum and is collected by one of the scrum halves to restart the game. The scrum is a relatively fast action in which a small number of players effectively reach a solution.

However, the CEO of IBM has about twenty direct reports. The CEO of the global market leader in cables, Prysmian, operates with twenty-five direct reports. In Luxottica, we count twenty. How can any one person listen to so many people? If each of these reports had an average of three strategic themes to discuss at each meeting, there would be about sixty issues to resolve in the case of IBM, Prysmian and Luxottica. The calculations are hypothetical, but the conclusion is very real. If there are too many first-line people, the decision-making process becomes complex and the likelihood of resilience falls. In fact, merely coordinating the diaries of twenty-five people to arrange a meeting can be a very complicated task.

Research indicates that the average number of people between the CEO and the base level has increased in the last two decades. Many CEOs appear to have surrounded themselves with more people in order to stand up to the ever-increasing pressure. Neilson and Wulf (2012) report that the average number of direct reports in firms has increased from 4.7 prior to 1990 to 9.8 today. Interestingly, the Volkswagen Group has reacted to the recent emissions scandal by announcing substantial change in its organizational model. Volkswagen will regroup its twelve brands into four clusters and name four regional heads to reduce the size of the management board, thereby creating a board that is less operational and more strategic. This is in line with our research, which suggests that organizational simplification helps increase the level of resilience. The CEO of Haier China, Zhang Rui Min, says: 'One of the reasons we move quickly is that we have few people at the top.'

Smaller teams also facilitate the building of informal networks and the creation of forms of 'clan control' (Ouchi, 1979). Clans rely on strong, direct relationships within the company and on continuous communication among employees. At the root of clans are common and shared interests and values. Iveco is one company that invests in forms of social control. Alfredo Altavilla, former CEO of Iveco, says: 'The idea is to have everyone around the table. If everyone controls everyone, the talented people are recognized.' In firms that have a large span of control (e.g. CEOs with twenty-five direct reports) clans (or 'inner circles') are sometimes created. However, if formal organizational structures are too distant from these informal structures, decision making becomes unnecessarily complicated. Therefore, we believe that from an organizational point of view, companies are more resilient when they: (1) simplify the organizational structure and thereby reduce span of control, and (2) put forms of social control into place, as described in the next section.

SOCIAL CONTROL

Our results suggest that resilient companies are organized according to a clan logic or, in other words, according to social-control mechanisms. The 'clan' is a structure in which relationships are mediated by high levels of feedback and collaboration, which entail trust and exchanges over an indefinite period (Ouchi, 1979). Clans imply social agreement on a wide range of values and beliefs. As they cannot rely on explicit market-price mechanisms, or on the explicit rules of bureaucracy and hierarchy, their ability to control organizational behaviour is based on a profound level of agreement among members regarding what constitutes 'correct' behaviour. This induces a high level of commitment from every member to socially prescribed behaviours (Ouchi, 1979).

Especially in times of great difficulty, confidence in the firm – in professional development or in a particularly motivating business climate – can induce acceptance of lower starting wages, greater instability of the external environment, a sense of insecurity about the future, giving rise to positive and stable performance in the long run. Equilibrium is obtained over time without a need for formalization. The clan recognizes and develops shared reference values, a common language and meanings, a sense of belonging, the loyalty of employees to the business community, and functional and divisional professional groups within the firm. Along these lines, the adoption of a clan orientation in the management of organizational relationships involves developing mechanisms that facilitate identifying the company's goals and its distinctive values. The corporate culture – its rituals, its history and its heroes – becomes a means of building and strengthening the clan. This culture is based on the participation and engagement of organizational members.

Many companies are developing informal control mechanisms based on engagement and horizontal communication. The leading Russian search engine, Yandex, holds a 64 per cent market share in Russia, which far exceeds Google's. It organized its headquarters in Moscow based on the dictates of extremely horizontal communication. A visitor to Yandex will find employees at all hierarchical levels working comfortably in flip-flops and shorts. The offices are almost all open spaces, while those organized for greater privacy have transparent glass doors that are usually open. Everyone can talk to everyone else. In fact, an employee who would like to take an idea to the CEO can do so without any problems. The offices are open 24 hours a day, and people can freely enter or leave at any time. A solarium allows for sunbathing, while 'multivitamin' rooms offer employees a continuous supply of fruit and vegetables.

EMC, a technology group (storage, big data, cloud) listed on the New York stock exchange, relies on the SIGM@ model, a model of grass-roots participation created by Marco Fanizzi, CEO and director of EMC Italia since 2011. Fanizzi says:

> SIGM@ stands for Sustainable Italian Growth Model. It is structured in five key areas: personal development, target, market, process improvement and community. The difference from other processes is its method: defining from below – with everyone's cooperation – areas of improvement; establishing the performance indicators to be monitored with those directly affected so as to understand the corrective actions needed; and delegating and empowering the project teams on the basis

of skills and roles. The rewards rest on merit-based criteria beyond the corporate function. We started with sample interviews of employees and have made them part of the decision-making process. Those interviews allowed us to identify fifty improvement projects. When anyone needs to discuss work progress, my door is always open.

(DataManager, 13 September 2013).[3]

Nokia was at the height of its success in the early 1990s when it entered the mobile-phone business. At the time, the organization had few employees, most of whom came from the same small town in Finland and had gone to school together. Most of Nokia's activities were based on trust and relationships.

Trust also achieves a great deal in very different contexts. This is demonstrated by Festivaletteratura di Mantova, a cultural event introduced in Mantua in early September 1997 that offers meetings with authors, readings, performances, concerts and art installations. The event, which was considered a great success by the public from the beginning, is currently among the most important literary and cultural events in Europe. The organizers were inspired by similar initiatives in Anglo-Saxon countries, and they have never hidden the fact that Festivaletteratura was inspired by a similar event in Hay-on-Wye in Wales. The peculiarity of this event is its small size – encounters between the audience and the authors take place within palaces, gardens and squares located in the historic city centre. The city itself becomes the frame of the events. Festivaletteratura has grown in terms of the number of events and the number of people attending. Fifteen thousand people took part in the 105 events held during the first Festivaletteratura in 1997. In 2012, 102,000 participated in 302 events. The organizing committee is still composed of Laura Baccaglioni, Carla Bernini, Annarosa Buttarelli, Francesco Caprini, Marcia Corraini, Luca Nicolini, Paolo Polettini and Gianni Tonelli. All eight members are from Mantua and know each other well. The strength of Festivaletteratura lies in its volunteers – people of all ages, mostly young men and women between the ages of fifteen and twenty-five, provide their time and energy to ensure the festival's success. After the initial years, Mantua also began to host volunteers from all across Italy and abroad. They are offered accommodation with families in Mantua and food from partner restaurants. Participation has skyrocketed – in 2004, there were more than 800 volunteers. The formula was consolidated and the success in the eyes of the public grew, but the ingredients

---

[3] See 'EMC. Metti i dati nel motore del tuo business' at: www.datamanager.it/rivista/emc-metti-i -dati-nel-motore-del-tuo-business-49638.html.

at the root of the event's popularity are those of the clan: people working together and sharing the same values.

ACCOUNTABILITY OF DECISION MAKING

As the external environment becomes more complex, problems multiply within the company and often quick solutions are required if the business is to survive. If decision making is shared and democratic, firms tend to refrain from clear and incisive decisions, and to shelter in compromises that do not harm anyone's position. All too often, conflict is avoided because it is time consuming, emotional and may not lead anywhere. In contrast, having a single person who holds final responsibility for decisions simplifies the situation and ensures that decisions are made. In a world that is rapidly changing, quick actions are required. Rarely do companies have months or years to consider an issue.

The Roman Empire is cited as an example of resilience in history (Carmeli and Markman, 2011). One reason the Empire was able to stand its ground for centuries was the decision-making power ultimately entrusted to a single leader, who would make decisions after hearing the opinions of the senate and the sages. The Roman Empire had to deal with numerous threats: barbarians at the gates, slaves in revolt, and increasingly complex bureaucracy and administration. Had the Empire not been able to decide quickly and efficiently, it would not have been the power it was, which flourished for more than four centuries.

If someone were to ask you, 'Can you push a piece of spaghetti across a table with your finger?' you would probably reply, 'It depends on whether the spaghetti is cooked.' If it is uncooked, it would be easy to push with a finger. If it is cooked, you would have to pull it. This metaphor explains the two situations in which a company can find itself. If the company is 'uncooked' – in a state of relative tranquillity and good health – change can be managed from behind with a degree of autonomy and without having to intervene greatly to get things going. If the company is 'cooked' – in a state of crisis or extreme complexity – decisions must be made from above and enforced, as a crisis is more easily resolved with centralized power. The second situation is the one in which we find ourselves today.

In the summer of 2013, Samsung placed three CEOs at the head of the company. The idea was to have a leader for each division: components, telecommunications and consumer products. The stock market seemed to receive the news relatively well and the share price rose by 2 per cent, probably because investors did not expect too many synergies between the divisions and preferred strong leadership with high autonomy in each division. However, some historical precedents suggest that companies that opt for shared leadership tend to develop problems. Blackberry is a case in point. In 2012, Mike Lazaridis and Jim Balsillie were appointed as Blackberry's co-CEOs. Under their guidance, Blackberry lost ground against Samsung and Apple. The main problems seemed to be the delay in the launch of the BlackBerry 10 and a global lack of customer service. In other words, having more than one CEO can lead to a type of paralysis. Dynamic companies cannot be governed by compromise.[4] The introduction of three CEOs is obviously also an expensive solution. In 2014, Samsung's three CEOs earned a total of KRW 21.89 billion (around EUR 17.5 million). However, due to poor results, their salaries were cut by more than 50 per cent to KRW 8.44 billion (around EUR 6.8 million) in 2015.

A survey carried out by the University of Missouri business school shows that even if markets generally welcome news of shared leadership, companies with dual leadership often encounter management problems. Professor Ferris of the University of Missouri says: 'The typical CEO has a dominant personality. If both individuals at the helm of a company want to be dominant, conflict ensues and nothing gets decided' (Arena, Ferris and Unlu, 2011). Hyundai Italia's CEO says, 'Things work because we know who must make the final decision. If this were not the case, we would be in chaos.'

DOES YOUR FIRM HAVE THE RIGHT CONTROL MODEL?

Our research suggests that the right organizational control model increases resilience and, in turn, produces SSP. To assess whether your firm has the right organizational control model, use this quick test. The various factors proposed can be evaluated on a scale from 1 to 5 (where 1 = strongly disagree and 5 = completely agree) and relate to resilience-related actions that can be introduced in the company. Of course, you are free to modify the tool and integrate the short questionnaire with other items or indicators that are already used to measure performance in various areas of the firm.

---

[4] Quentin Fottrell: 'Does Samsung really need three CEOs?' at: www.marketwatch.com/story/are -two-or-three-ceos-better-than-one-2013-03-20.

Table 9.1 Assess your firm's control model

	Strongly disagree				Completely agree
	1	2	3	4	5
In my organization, the higher levels take the time to personally communicate with the operational base.					
In my organization, there are few people who assume final responsibility for decisions.					
Top management shows interest in all employees without looking at the hierarchical level.					
In my organization, members of top management are often present in the company.					
Organizational mechanisms score (the average of the four answers)					
Reference grid	1–2: Low resilience. You are not prepared for external shocks and need to invest in a resilience programme.				
	3: Average resilience. Identify blind resilience spots and work on them.				
	4–5: High resilience. Stay the course. Make sure you stay alert.				

Source: Adapted from Thomas and McDaniel (1990).

CHAPTER 10

Conclusion

In this book, we have analysed how 705 firms from different industries have reacted to a crisis or a series of external shocks. What emerges is a model that can help firms build a strategy, organization and culture that is more resilient. We have shown that firms can and should measure their resilience, and that they should invest time and resources in increasing their resilience to the desired level. Firms are not naturally resilient – they have to be made resilient. Think about children in their first year of life. Most of them hardly get sick because their anxious parents protect them from any possible environmental influence. However, when they start in pre-school, they frequently get sick. This happens because they do not yet have strong immunity defences, which must be built. The same applies to businesses. A firm is not born resilient – it grows into resilience.

We have argued that resilience is the ability to withstand crises and deliver sustained superior performance (SSP). Our resilience model (see Figure 10.1) encompasses seven core drivers of resilience that support the process of making the firm more resilient.

Step 1: Take into Consideration Resilience by Creating Industry Foresight

At the start of every strategic process, a sense of urgency must be created around the central issues. Before investing time in measuring and managing resilience, we need to address managers' concerns in relation to resilience. They might, for example, ask: Why should we raise our resilience level if we are evaluated on the basis of quarterly earnings? The reductions in short-term profitability associated with investing in resilience may be just one concern managers have. Such issues have to be addressed to arrive at a consensus on the importance of increasing the capacity to absorb shocks. Stakeholders are not necessarily interested in firms that are able to absorb shocks. In publicly listed companies, for example, investors usually like growth stories and expect

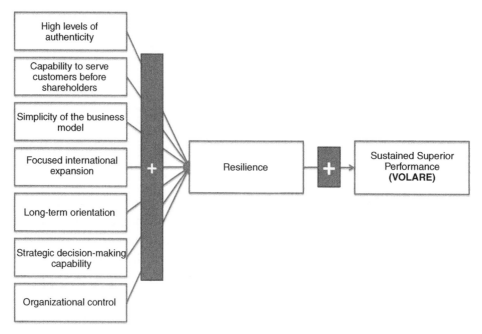

Figure 10.1 The drivers of resilience
Source: authors' own

high short-term profitability. They are also usually the first to understand the performance implications of market changes and allocate their capital accordingly. Investors' resiliency comes from a diversified portfolio and effective asset allocation. This leads to a few key questions: Why do we want stable firms? What is the cost of fragility?

We have argued that resilient companies have relatively high, stable profits over time, which leads to higher shareholder returns in the long run. Therefore, any manager should be genuinely interested in greater resiliency. In addition, we believe that fragile companies generally have to borrow money at higher interest rates, attract less talented people, and are not at the top of the list for strategic partnerships with suppliers and customers. We are not suggesting that firms should avoid risky projects. On the contrary, entrepreneurs – by definition – make decisions under conditions of uncertainty and make a profit because they take risks. However, we argue that firms that operate at higher levels of risk should compensate their owners with higher returns. Resilient firms are able to generate higher returns than their peers with similar risk profiles.

Nevertheless, we also point out that the bigger or more successful the firm, the more difficult it is to motivate its management team to think about resilience. In 1990, Joseph Tainter wrote a book called *The Collapse of Complex Societies* (Tainter, 1990) in which he describes the origins and decline of many societies, including the Roman Empire, the Mayans and the Phoenicians. All of these cultures followed the same path: they arrived at a certain level of sophistication, became bigger, thrived, increased in complexity and, at the height of their development, collapsed in a relatively short period of time. These societies originally thrived because they found themselves with an abundance of resources, an abundance created by a mix of a favourable geographical position, good internal organization and luck. Management of this surplus increased the complexity of the situation (e.g. agricultural techniques improved, new machines were built). The complexity rapidly turned into rigidity, such that doing small things became impossible because the entire organizational machinery had to be mobilized.

Scenario techniques may help motivate the management teams of large organizations to think about resilience. We have become used to the notion of stress tests in the financial-services industry. Such tests help managers understand whether their firm would survive under very adverse conditions. The same needs to be done for firms in other industries. Scenarios are coherent descriptions of alternative hypothetical futures that reflect different perspectives of past, present and future developments, which can serve as a basis for action. Scenario development aims to combine analytical knowledge with creative thinking in an effort to capture a wide range of possible future developments. Scenario techniques expand the thought process to envisage a wider range of possible futures with the goals of challenging the prevailing mind-set and identifying early warning signals.

The concept of 'foresight', as described by Hamel and Prahalad (1994), refers to an attempt to go beyond the creation of scenarios. In these authors' views, 'competing for industry foresight' is essentially competition for 'intellectual leadership', which allows a company to envisage the future. In this way, a company may gain control over the evolution of its industry, which is mainly characterized by three factors: (1) types of future customer benefits, (2) the competences needed to offer those benefits and (3) the configuration of the customer interface (1994, p. 73). Foresight is developed through eclecticism, a liberal use of analogy and metaphor, an inherent contrarianism, the desire to guide the customer and a genuine empathy for human needs. Foresight is the product of a childlike innocence about what could be and should be, as well as curiosity and speculation (1994, p. 82–3). In sum, the quest for industry foresight is the quest to develop a 'gut feeling' for what does not yet exist.

Hamel and Prahalad (1994) apply the term 'foresight' slightly differently from the way in which it has been used in the relevant literature. In the field of futures studies, foresight is seen as a human capacity and skill that is deployed in many ways and protects people from making certain mistakes. As such, it is a mental process (Slaughter, 1993, p. 293). A typical example of foresight is taking out an umbrella before leaving the house in case it starts to rain. Richard Slaughter (1993, p. 293) distinguishes foresight from mere prediction and forecasting. A prediction is a confident statement about the future state of affairs, and is best confined to systems that can be fully measured or understood. Forecasts are based on the careful analysis of the past and 'if … then' relations are constructed and extrapolated into the future. The concept of foresight is again distinct from forecasts:

> Foresight involves a conscious effort to expand awareness and to clarify the dynamics of emerging situations. The foresight principle is called into play by irreducible uncertainties created by the precariousness of life. Foresight is 'common sense' in that there is obvious merit in seeking to avoid dangers and reduce risks. However, the principle is easier to implement on the individual level than at the social level.
>
> (Slaughter, 1990, p. 801)

Hence, foresight has not always been a means to create the future, as Hamel and Prahalad imply. It is more frequently used to express the human ability to foresee the future in order to protect oneself from harm. However, sometimes there is no way to predict large-scale shocks. These events become 'black swans' (Taleb, 2007); a term taken from the Latin poet Juvenal. The expression was used in philosophical discussions in ancient Rome to indicate a fact that is virtually impossible to realise. It was based on the presumption that 'all swans are white', an assertion that made sense until the discovery of the Australian black swan. It is impossible to foresee the future of a complex system with free agents. If an organization is looked upon as a complex adaptive system – a system that produces changeable and diverse order, and one in which behaviour is not deterministic and cannot be predicted – then foresight changes its nature. Foresight has to be reduced to the mere recognition of patterns in a stream of self-organizing, spontaneous action with emerging order (Stacey 1993). In fact, Stacey states that 'free systems cannot have much in the way of foresight and hence cannot be "in control"' (p. 189). Consequently, it might be impossible to develop foresight at all. Instead of searching for foresight, it might be more meaningful to follow McDermott's suggestion of dealing with the problem of living without foresight (McDermott, 1996, p. 194).

We do not go as far as Stacey, as we believe that there are events that one can predict with a reasonable level of accuracy. However, there will always be events that cannot be predicted. The *Harvard Business Review* cover of October 2015 included the headline: 'The new rules of competition: be paranoid, disrupt yourself, go to war for talent'. Firms have to invest time in understanding the future and they must prepare for the unexpected with the intellectual courage to reveal evidence outside the actual way of thinking. They must also have an ability to hold two conflicting ideas in mind without losing the power to function. Finally, they would benefit from a good dose of scepticism when faced with conventional wisdom. The creation of foresight and, thereby, of a sense of urgency with regard to protective measures is the first step in our resilience-building programme.

Step 2: Identify Your Resilience Level and Choose Your Target

As a next step, we need to understand the extent to which a firm is currently resilient. Scenarios and industry foresight serve as the basis for assessing the robustness of core competences and allow firms to develop a risk/return profile for strategic options. In other words, if you have developed industry foresight, you get a good feeling for how well prepared your firm is to absorb external shocks or to drive industry change. Complementary to developing foresight, management teams can be motivated to invest in a resilience programme by measuring how resilient the company was in the past. We have presented VO-LARE as a proxy for resilience and as a new performance measure. While we have developed a measure of firm resilience that complements existing performance measures, we do not criticize traditional accounting practices or the use of prevailing performance measures per se. Accounting and financial measures, and the quantification of performance in terms of earnings and revenue growth, cash flow or debt load are clearly paramount. A firm's financial performance allows decision makers to assess the firm's strategies and activities in objective monetary terms. We worry, however, about the misapplication of traditional performance measures for the purpose of gauging firm resilience. In other words, measures that were designed, optimized and validated as quarterly and yearly financial performance parameters are not quite suitable for gauging a firm's ten-year resilience.

Firm performance matters. High performance attracts and motivates top talent; creates access to resources for growth and for fending off competition; serves as a gateway to critical partners, suppliers and buyers; and provides cash outlays for international expansion, R & D, and innovation. Conversely, underperformance can set off waves of creative destruction with devastating chain reactions. The inclusion of VOLARE in the set of performance indicators that guide investment decisions and communicate performance will increase the amount of attention top management pays to long-term risk and return objectives. It will also allow managers to justify investments in 'shock absorbers' like higher cash reserves, a focus on geographical and product scope, and the development of a larger pool of top talent to quickly shift resources to more attractive opportunities.

It is easy to calculate VOLARE if you are not obsessed with statistically robust results and can accept a rough indication of your level of resilience: take the return on equity (ROE) of your peers in the past six to ten years, calculate the average (return) and the standard deviation (risk), and plot the results on a chart. You may want to adjust for outliers that have a high standard deviation due to constantly improving results. Next, identify the highest ROE points for given risk intervals and connect them with a curve. This line represents the VOLARE 10 curve – the benchmark for your industry. All firms along this line showed the highest resilience in the period you analysed, but they have different risk/return profiles. You then shift the curve down in a way to derive a VOLARE scale from 0 to 10.

Step 3: Identify and Evaluate Resilience Drivers

You now have a list of comparable firms in your industry with resilience scores, and you can begin to understand why some firms have higher scores and why some score low. We have undertaken these calculations for more than 700 firms from seven industries, and came up with the resilience model shown above. The model lists seven drivers of resilience. When further investigating your own industry, you may find that other drivers are more important. You can then modify the model. We do not claim that the model is complete or applicable to all industries to the same degree.

For example, we suggest that focused international expansion increases the resilience of firms. However, we have a hard time stating what we really mean by 'focused'. What is the right level of international expansion? In Chapter 6, we argued that the extant research does not offer a clear answer to the question of how international expansion affects a firm's profitability. For retail banks, food producers or law firms, international expansion offers fewer benefits than for producers of aeroplane engines or flat screens. However, there are a few suggestions in relation to the degree of international expansion that we feel confident in generalizing: (1) in most industries, there is a minimal critical scale that firms have to reach to be able to compete; (2) this minimal critical scale has moved in recent years to a higher level; (3) many firms overestimate the economies of scale and scope that increased geographical and product diversification generates; (4) firms should invest in and maintain a strong core (home) market or region as a source of strength; and (5) firms should develop a methodology to selectively invest in coherent geographical areas.

These are the results of our study in relation to international expansion and resilience. However, the results may be different in your industry. We therefore suggest that you organize a resilience workshop in which you discuss the list of best and worst VOLARE performers in your industry, and then develop your own conclusions on how to increase resilience. The set of questions that we offer for assessing each resilience driver is a good place to start. We encourage you to modify the quick tests and integrate them with the indicators that you already use in your firm. How do you measure customer centricity? Do you use a 'net promotor score' (i.e. asking customers: How likely are you to recommend us to a friend?). Integrate the results of your survey with your resilience scorecard.

In the previous chapters, we proposed a self-assessment tool for each driver of resilience, which gives a score for each driver. When all of the driver

Table 10.1 Overall resilience score

Authenticity score	
Customer-centricity score	
Product-focus score	
Market-focus score	
Long-term orientation score	
Decision-making ability score	
Organizational mechanisms score	
Total resilience score (average of the individual scores)	
Reference grid	1–2: Low resilience. You are not prepared for external shocks and need to invest in a resilience programme.
	3: Average resilience. Identify blind resilience spots and work on them.
	4–5: High resilience. Stay the course. Make sure you stay alert.

assessments have been completed, the different scores should be added together to arrive at the total resilience score for the company. In other words, by transcribing the individual scores tallied at the end of chapters 4–9 and averaging them, you can calculate your company's overall resilience score.

Step 4: Implement a Resilience Programme

After you have a good idea of what makes your firm resilient and what makes it fragile, you can start to improve resilience. The results of the check-up will highlight necessary courses of action. Unfortunately, too many firms start implementing necessary changes too late. Think about how divestment decisions are made in your firm. How good is your firm at quickly shifting attention and financial resources from one area to another? Do you have a structured process for downscaling or selling off troubled businesses? Resilient firms sell units before they must.

Such change usually gives rise to strong emotions, especially as there is no apparent need for such strong measures. Change is usually introduced if either the pressure exerted by forces for change increases or the barriers to change are dismantled. An increase in the pressure for change often leads to increased resistance and can therefore be a zero-sum game. Therefore, barriers to change must be accurately identified and purposefully dismantled. In 1963, Kurt Lewin suggested a three-stage process for modifying organizations: unfreeze – change – refreeze.

This is an easy principle to understand but it is difficult to implement. In the first phase (unfreeze), a sense of urgency regarding the main areas of change needs to be established. As change involves pain, the pain associated with not changing needs to be increased. One way of getting the organization's full attention is to deliberately engender a crisis, as a feeling of security often predominates, particularly in large companies. In such situations, the dominant thought seems to be: 'Headquarters will simply have to release a bit more money because things are not going well for us at the moment.' Even more difficult to handle is the attitude that: 'Everything's going fine for us. Why do we need to change?' The use of shock tactics to shake up the organization can help prepare employees for change initiatives. Obviously, it is inadvisable to resort to these tactics too often, or to further frighten already intimidated and insecure staff.

A sense of crisis can be provoked through the use of actual figures from (struggling) company accounts, through direct feedback from unsatisfied customers or through warnings regarding the increasing strength of the competition. Alternatively, a five-minute time-lapse video demonstrating the changing geography of the Roman Empire – showing how a great empire can arise over a period of more than four minutes and then fall apart in a few seconds – can also be very effective. Managers might follow these tactics with examples of the rise and decline of such companies such as AEG or *Encyclopædia Britannica*, which they can use to talk about how changes in the industry may affect the firm.

To add credibility to a change initiative, the company must move away from the status quo and from status symbols related to past successes. Company cars with chauffeurs, luxuriously outfitted executive offices or business lounges for top management all give the staff the impression that everything is ok. The publication of new organizational charts will be insufficient for producing fundamental change in a company or for implementing far-reaching strategic initiatives. Change processes are frequently inefficient or ineffective. Imagine a large, barren tree in the winter that is filled with a large number of happily settled crows. An angry farmer tries to drive the crows away by shooting at the tree with a gun, which forces the birds into the air. They circle over the tree and return after a few minutes. Most of them are sitting on different branches and a few lie dead on the ground. Did anything fundamentally change? To keep the process of change from operating in this manner, programmes to modify the company's processes, management composition and value system are necessary.

It might be helpful to consider starting a resilience programme at the beginning of a new chapter in a company's strategic development. Why do people decide to give up smoking on 1 January rather than on 14 August? They need a point in time at which they can say that one chapter is closed and that there is an opportunity to start a new one. A radical alteration in workplace conditions or a move into new offices can create such a restart effect. Only when a large part of the organization is ready for change can the alterations be pursued in a purposeful manner. Although we have argued that we live in a world of high volatility and constant change, we believe that fundamental, deep change cannot be undertaken too frequently. People and organizations need routines, which are what makes them efficient. Therefore, we need the third phase (refreeze) to ensure development of the routines necessary for dealing with day-to-day business.

Bibliography

Alimehmeti, G. and Paletta, A. (2012) Ownership concentration and effects over firm performance: Evidence from Italy, *European Scientific Journal*, October edition, **8**(22), 39–49.

Arbesman, S. (2012) *The Half-life of Facts*. New York, NY: Current.

Arena, M., Ferris, S. and Unlu, E. (2011) It Takes Two: The Incidence and Effectiveness of Co-CEOs, *Financial Review*, **46**(3), 385–412.

Arnold, G. (2008) *Corporate Financial Management*. Pearson Education Limited, Harlow, England.

Ata, Z. and Toker, A. (2012) The Effect of Customer Relationship Management Adoption in Business-to-business Markets, *Journal of Business and Industrial Marketing*, **27**(6), 497–507.

Balu, R. (2001) How to Bounce Back from Setbacks, *Fast Company*, **45** (April), 148–56.

Bauman, Z. (2009) *Modernità e globalizzazione*, Roma, Edizioni dell'Asino.

Barker III, V.L. and Duhaime, I.M. (1997) Change in the Turnaround Process: Theory and Empirical Evidence, *Strategic Management Journal*, **18**(1), 13–38 (p. 20).

Barnett, C.K. and Pratt, M.G. (2000) From Threat-rigidity to Flexibility – Toward a Learning Model of Autogenic Crisis in Organisations, *Journal of Organisational Change Management*, **13**(1), 74–88.

Barney, J.B. (1991) Firm Resources and Sustained Competitive Advantage, *Journal of Management*, **17**(1), 99–120.

Briguglio, L., Cordina, G., Farrugia, N. and Vella, S. (2008) Economic Vulnerability and Resilience Concepts and Measurements, Unu-Wider, Research Paper n. 2008/55.

Buyl, T., Boone, C., Hendriks, W. and Matthyssens, P. (2011) Top Management Team Functional Diversity and Firm Performance: The Moderating Role of CEO Characteristics, *Journal of Management Studies*, **48**(1), 151–77.

Carmeli, A. and Markman, G.D. (2011) Capture, Governance, and Resilience: Strategy Implications from the History of Rome, *Strategic Management Journal*, **32**(3), 322–41.

Carroll, G. and Wheaton, D.R. (2009) The Organisational Construction of Authenticity: An Examination of Contemporary Food and Dining in the U.S., *Organisational Behavior*, **29**, 255–82.

Casey, B.J., Somerville, L.H., Gotlib, I.H., Ayduk, O., Franklin, N.T., Askren, M.K., Jonides, J., Berman, M.G., Wilson, N.L., Teslovich, T., Glover, G., Zayas, V., Mischel, W. and Shoda, Y. (2011) Behavioral and Neural Correlates of Delay of Gratification 40 Years Later, *Proceedings of the National Academy of Sciences* (PNAS), **108**(36), 14998–5003.

Chatterjee, S. and Wernerfelt, B. (1991) The Link between Resources and Type of Diversification: Theory and Evidence, *Strategic Management Journal*, **12**(1), 33–48.

Christensen, C.M. (1997) *The Innovator's Dilemma: When New Technologies Cause Great Firms to Fail*. Boston, MA: Harvard Business Publishing.

Clark, P.E. and Wilson, J. (1961) Incentive System: A Theory of Organisation, *Administrative Science Quarterly*, **6**, 129–66.

Coleman, J.S. (1988) Social Capital in the Creation of Human Capital, *The American Journal of Sociology*, **94** (supplement), S95–S120.

Conant, J., Mokwa, M. and Varadarajan, R. (2006) Strategic Types, Distinctive Marketing Competencies and Organisational Performance: A Multiple Measures-Based Study, *Strategic Management Journal*, **11**(5), 365–83.

Coutu, D.L. (2002) How Resilience Works, *Harvard Business Review*, May, 46–55.

Covey, S.R. (1989) *The Seven Habits of Highly Effective People*. London: Simon and Schuster.

Dallocchio, M. and Vizzaccaro, M. (forthcoming) *Valorizzazione del territorio e sviluppo delle eccellenze locali – Il saper fare italiano per il rilancio dell'economia*.

Dallocchio M., Lussan, F. and Vizzaccaro, M. (forthcoming) l'Internazionalizzazione dell'eccellenza italiana.

Dunning, J. (1988) The Eclectic Paradigm of International Production: A Restatement and Some Possible Extensions, *Journal of International Business Studies*, **19**, 1–31.

Edwards, W. (1954) The Theory of Decision Making, *Psychological Bulletin*, **51**(4), 380–417.

Eggers, F., Dwyer, M., Kraus, S., Vallaster, C. and Güldenberg, S. (2013) The Impact of Brand Authenticity on Brand Trust and SME Growth: A CEO Perspective, *Journal of World Business*, **48**(3), 340–48.

Eisenhardt, K.M. and Graebner, M.E. (2007) Theory Building from Cases: Opportunities and Challenges, *Academy of Management Journal*, **50**, 25–32.

Eisenhardt, K.M. and Sull, D. (2001) Strategy as Simple Rules, *Harvard Business Review*, January.

Fine, G.A. (2001) *Difficult Reputations: Collective Memories of the Evil, Inept, and Controversial*. Chicago, IL: University of Chicago Press.

Freeman, S.F., Hirschhorn, L. and Maltz, M. (2004) Organisation Resilience and Moral Purpose: Sandler O'Neill and Partners in the Aftermath of 9/11/01, Paper Presented at the National Academy of Management Meetings, New Orleans.

Fredrickson, B.L., Tugade, M.M., Waugh, C.E. and Larkin, G.R. (2003) What Good Are Positive Emotions in Crisis? A Prospective Study of Resilience and Emotions following the Terrorist Attacks on the United States on September 11th, 2001, *Journal of Personality and Social Psychology*, **84**(2), 365–76.

Frery, F. (2006) The Fundamental Dimensions of Strategy, *MIT Sloan Management Review*, **48**, 71–5.

Gedajlovic, E. and Shapiro, D. (2002) Ownership and Firm Profitability in Japan, *Academy of Management Journal*, **45**(3), 575–85.

Geringer, J.M., Beamish, P.W. and da Costa, R.C. (1989) Diversification Strategy and Internationalization, *Strategic Management Journal*, **10**, 109–19.

Grant, R.M. (1987) Multinationality and Performance among British Manufacturing Companies, *Journal of International Business Studies*, **18**(3), 79–89.

Gittell, J.H., Cameron, K., Lim, S. and Rivas, V. (2006) Relationships, Layoffs, and Organisational Resilience: Airline Industry Responses to September 11th, *Journal of Applied Behavioral Science*, **42**(3), 300–30.

Gubitta, P. and Giannecchini, M. (2002) Governance e Flessibilità nelle PMI del Nordest, *Family Business Review*, **25**(4), 277–99.

Gulati, R. (2010) *Reorganize for Resilience: Putting Customers at the Center of Your Business*. Boston, MA: Harvard Business Review Press.

Gummesson, E. (2008) Extending the Service-dominant Logic: From Customer Centricity to Balanced Centricity, *Journal of the Academy of Marketing Science*, **36**(1), 15–17.

Hackman, J.R. (1987) 'The Design of Work Teams' in J. W. Lorsch (ed), *Handbook of Organisational Behavior*, Upper Saddle River, NJ: Prentice-Hall, pp. 215–342.

Hamel, G. and Prahalad C.K. (1994) *Competing for the Future*, Boston, MA: Harvard Business Review Press.

Hammond, J.S., Keeney, R.L and Raiffa, H. (2006) The Hidden Traps in Decision Making, *Harvard Business Review*, January.

Heidegger, M. (1927) *Being and Time*, trans. J. Macquarrie and E.S. Robinson. New York, NY: Harper and Row.

Hitt, M., Hoskisson, R. and Kim, H. (1997) International Diversification: Effects on Innovation and Firm Performance in Product-Diversified Firms, *Academy of Management Journal*, **40**(4), 767–98.

Hoenen, A.K. and Venzin, M. (2013) *Transforming Carlsberg into a Cosmopolitan Firm: Building Strategy Process Capabilities*. Cranfield: The Case Centre.

Holling, C. (1973), Resilience and Stability of Ecological Systems, *Annual Review of Ecology and Systematics*, **4**, 1–23.

Hoskisson, R., Hitt, M., Johnson, R. and Moesel, D. (1993) Construct Validity of an Objective (Entropy) Categorical Measure of Diversification Strategy, *Strategic Management Journal*, **14**, 215–35.

Isenberg, D. (1984) How Managers Think, *Harvard Business Review*, November–December.

Jamrog, J.J., McCann, J.E., Lee, J.M., Morrison, C.L., Selsky, J.W. and Vickers, M. (2006) *Agility and Resilience in the Face of Continuous Change*. New York, NY: American Management Association.

Kachaner N., Stalk, G. and Block A. (2012) What You Can Learn from Family Business, *Harvard Business Review*, November.

Kahneman, D. and Tversky, A. (1979) Prospect Theory: An Analysis of Decisions under Risk, *Econometrica*, **47**(2), 313–27.

Kaplan, S.N and Minton, B.A. (2012) How Has CEO Turnover Changed?, *International Review of Finance*, **12**(1), 57–87.

Kipnis, D. and Lane, W.D. (1982) Self-confidence and Leadership, *Journal of Applied Psychology*, **46**, 291–5.

Kontinen, T. and Ojala, A. (2012) 'Internationalization Pathways among Family-Owned SMEs, *International Marketing Review*, **29**(5), 496–518.

Kotter, J. and Heskett, J. (1992) *Corporate Culture and Performance*, New York, NY: Macmillan.

Lengnick-Hall, M.L., Beck, T.E. and Lengnick-Hall, C.A. (2011) Developing a Capacity for Organisational Resilience through Strategic Human Resource Management, *Human Resource Management Review*, **21**, 243–55.

Lewis, M. (2004) *Moneyball: The Art of Winning an Unfair Game*. New York, NY: W.W. Norton and Company.

Lichtenstein, S. and Slovic, P. (1971) Reversals of Preference between Bids and Choices in Gambling Decisions, *Journal of Experimental Psychology*, **89**, 46–55.

Llewellyn, D.T. (2002) *The Future for Small and Regional Banks in Europe*, Vienna: Société Universitaire Européenne de Recherches Financières.

Lu, J.W. and Beamish, P.W. (2001) The Internationalization and Performance of SMEs, *Strategic Management Journal*, **22**, 565–86.

Markowitz, H.M. (1959) *Portfolio Selection: Efficient Diversification of Investments*. New York, NY: Wiley.

Markman, G. and Venzin, M. (2014) Resilience: Lessons from Banks That Have Braved the Economic Crisis – and from Those That Have Not, *International Business Review*, **23**(6), 1096–107.

Martin, R. (2010) The Age of Customer Capitalis, *Harvard Business Review*, January–February, 36–77.

Mauboussin, M.J. (2012) The Big Idea. The True Measures of Success, *Harvard Business Review*, October.

McGrath R.G. (2013) Transient advantage. *Harvard Business Review*, June.

McDermott, B. (1996) Foresight Is an Illusion. *Long Range Planning*, **29**(2), 195–202.

Mezzadri, A. (2005) *Il passaggio del testimone. Sedici casi di successo in imprese familiari italiane*. Milan: Franco Angeli.

Miller, D.J. (2004), Firms' Technological Resources and the Performance Effects of Diversification: A Longitudinal Study, *Strategic Management Journal*, **25** (11), 1097–19.

Mintzberg, H. (1975) The Manager's Job: Folklore and Fact, *Harvard Business Review*, July–August.

Mueller, J. (2012) Why Individuals in Larger Teams Perform Worse, *Organisational Behavior and Human Decision Processes*, **117**(1), 111–24.

Neilson, G.L. and Wulf, J. (2012) How Many Direct Reports? *Harvard Business Review*, April, 112–19.

Ouchi, W.G. (1979) A Conceptual Framework for the Design of Organisational Control Mechanisms, *Management Science*, **25**(9), 833–48.

Palich, L.E., Cardinal, L.B. and Miller, C.C. (2000) Curvilinearity in the Diversification–Performance Linkage: An Examination of Over Three Decades of Research, *Strategic Management Journal*, **21**(2), 155–74.

Parada, P., Alemany, L. and Planellas, M. (2009) The Internationalisation of Retail Banking: Banco Santander's Journey towards Globalisation, *Long Range Planning*, **42**, 654–77.

Perlow, L., Okhuysen, G. and Repenning, N. (2002) The Speed Trap: Exploring the Relationship between Decision Making and Temporal Context, *Academy of Management Journal*, **4.1**(5), 931–55.

Pfeffer, J. (2013) Power, Capriciousness, and Consequences, *Harvard Business Review,* April.

Pintea, M.O. (2012) Performance Evaluation: Literature Review and Time Evolution, *Annals of the University of Oradea, Economic Science Series*, **21**(1), 753.

Pirotti, G.B. (2013) Quando la crisi diventa opportunità e a farsi spazio in Italia è un'azienda cinese. A colloquio con Enrico Ligabue, *Economia & Management*, **2**(2), 75–78.

Pirotti, G.B. and Venzin, M. (2014) Come le aziende possono resistere e reagire in tempo di crisi: misurare e rinforzare la resilienza organizzativa, *Economia & Management*, **1**, 59–74.

Prahalad, C.K. and Hamel, G. (1990) The Core Competence of the Corporation, *Harvard Business Review,* May–June, 79–91.

Robbins, S. (1998) *Organisational Behaviour: Concepts, Controversies, Applications*, Upper Saddle River, NJ: Prentice-Hall.

Rochester Business Journal (2017) www.rbj.net/article.asp?aID=190212, 27 January.

Rosenzweig, P. (2007) Misunderstanding the Nature of Company Performance: The Halo Effect and Other Business Delusions, *California Management Review*, **49**(4), 6–20.

Ross, B. (2009) Ten Tips to Winning at Consumer Centricity: For Retailers and Manufacturers, *Journal of Consumer Marketing*, **26**(6), 450–54.

Rudolph, J.W. and Repenning, N.P. (2002) Disaster Dynamics: Understanding the Role of Quantity in Organisational Collapse, *Administrative Science Quarterly*, **47**, 1–30.

Rumelt, R.P. (1974) *Strategy, Structure, and Economic Performance*, Boston, MA: Harvard Business School, Division of Research.

Rumelt, R.P. (1982) Diversification Strategy and Profitability, *Strategic Management Journal*, **3**(4), 359–69.

Sartre, J.P. (1943) *Being and Nothingness: An Essay on Phenomenological Ontology*, trans. Barnes H. New York, NY: Philosophical Library, 1956.

Seligman, M. (2011) Building Resilience, *Harvard Business Review*, April.

Slaughter, R.A. (1990) The Foresight Principle, *Futures*, **22**(8), 801–19.

Slaughter, R.A. (1993) Futures Concepts, *Futures*, April, 289–314.

Simons, R. (2000) *Performance Measurement and Control Systems for Implementing Strategy: Text and Cases*. Upper Saddle River, NJ: Prentice Hall.

Sirmon, D.G. and Hitt, M.A. (2003) Managing Resources: Linking Unique Resources, Management and Wealth Creation in Family Firms, *Entrepreneurship Theory and Practice*, **27**, 339–58.

Sharot, T. (2012) *Optimism Bias*. London: Constable and Robinson.

Shiu, E., Walsh, G., Shaw, D. and Hassan, L. (2011) Consumer Uncertainty, Revisited, *Psychology and Marketing*, **28**(6), 584–607.

Shleifer, A. and Vishny, R.W. (1997) A Survey of Corporate Governance, *The Journal of Finance*, **LII**(2), 737–783.

Stacey, R.D. (1993) *Strategic Management and Organizational Dynamics*, London: Pitman Publishing Inc.

Sull, D. (2009) How to Thrive in Turbulent Markets, *Harvard Business Review*, February.

Sullivan, D. (1994) Measuring the Degree of Internationalization of a Firm, *Journal of International Business Studies*, **25**(2), 325–42.

Sutcliffe, K.M. and Vogus, T.J. (2003) 'Organizing for Resilience' in K.S. Cameron, J.E. Dutton and R.E. Quinn (eds), *Positive Organisational*

Scholarship: Foundations of a New Discipline, San Francisco, CA: Berrett-Koehler, pp. 94–110.

Schweiger, D.M., Sandberg, W.R. and Ragan, J.R. (1986) Group Approaches for Improving Strategic Decision Making: A Comparative Analysis of Dialectical Inquiry, Devil's Advocacy, and Consensus, *The Academy of Management Journal*, **29**(1), 51–71.

Tainter, J. (1990) *The Collapse of Complex Societies*. Cambridge: Cambridge University Press.

Taleb, N.N. (2007) *The Black Swan: The Impact of the Highly Improbable*. New York, NY: Random House.

Tallman, S. and Li, J. (1996) Effects of International Diversity and Product Diversity on the Performance of Multinational Firms, *Academy of Management Journal*, **39**, 179–96.

Thomas, J.B. and McDaniel, J.R.R. (1990) Interpreting Strategic Issues: Effects of Strategy and the Information-Processing Structure of Top Management Teams, *Academy of Management Journal*, **33**, 286–306.

Trabucchi, P. (2007) 'I resist therefore I am', Milan: Corbaccio.

Towers, S. (2010) *Outside-In. The Secret of the 21st Century Leading Companies*. BP Group Press, London.

Tversky, A. (1969) Intransitivity of Preferences, *Psychological Review*, **76**, 31–48.

Venzin, M. (2004) *La gestione strategica delle aziende multinazionali*. Milan: Egea.

Venzin, M. (2005) *The Strategy Process*, English translation of the book *Der Strategieprozess: Analyse – Planung – Umsetzung* (with Carsten Rasner and Volker Mahnke), Cyan Campus.

Weick, K. and Sutcliffe K. (2007) *Managing the Unexpected: Resilient Performance in an Age of Uncertainty*. San Francisco, CA: Jossey Bass.

Werner, E.E. (1982) Vulnerable but Invincible: High Risk Children from Birth to Adulthood, *European Child and Adolescent Psychiatry*, **5**(1), supplement, 47–51.

Zahra, S.A. (2003) International Expansion of U.S. Manufacturing Family Businesses: The Effect of Ownership and Involvement, *Journal of Business Venturing*, **18**(4), 495–512.

Zahra, S.A., Neubaum, D.O. and Huse, M. (2000) Entrepreneurship in Medium-size Companies: Exploring the Effects of Ownership and Governance Systems, *Journal of Management*, **26**(5), 947–76.

Zolli, A. and Healey, A.M. (2012) *Resilience: Why Things Bounce Back*. New York, NY: Simon and Schuster.

Index